Dance and Its Audience
Appreciating the Art of Movement

Tami White

Published by The Educational Publisher, Inc.
Biblio Publishing
www.BiblioPublishing.com
1313 Chesapeake Ave
Columbus, OH 43212
ISBN: 978-1-62249-092-9

Contents

A Note to Instructors

This book was designed for use in a one-semester dance appreciation survey class. As such, I have attempted to limit the information provided to that which can be covered comfortably. This means that many noteworthy choreographers and dancers do not appear in this text. Teachers may wish to add other important contributors to the art of dance, particularly in Chapters five, six, and seven. I welcome your comments and feedback on this first edition, which can be made via email to tmwhite@odu.edu.

Tami M. White is an adjunct faculty member with the Dance Department at Old Dominion University in Norfolk, VA. A graduate of the Virginia Governor's School for the Arts, she holds B.A. and M.S.Ed. degrees from Old Dominion University and an Ed.D. from the University of Virginia.

Acknowledgements

I would like to thank my fellow teachers at Old Dominion University, particularly Marilyn Marloff and Amanda Kinzer, for their assistance in preparing this work. I also thank Deborah Thorpe at the Governor's School for the Arts for encouraging me in the field of dance and beyond. I dedicate this book to my parents, Louis and Susan Marconyak, for their endless support of my dance endeavors, and to my family, Brad, Susan, and Gunner White, for giving me two nights a week to do what I love.

Cover Photo

Cover photography was taken by Katie Tuebner and features dancers Amy Scaringe and Wayles Haynes.

Chapter 1

Introduction

What is dance? Webster's dictionary defines dance as "a series of rhythmic and patterned bodily movements usually performed to music." Must dance always be performed to music? How much of the body must be moving in order for us to consider the movement a dance? Perhaps more helpful is to look at Webster's definition of art: "the conscious use of skill and creative imagination especially in the production of aesthetic objects." Rather than producing aesthetic objects, however, dancers and choreographers create aesthetic movement.

Take a moment to consider your own exposure to dance. Most people have participated in dance at a club, party, or wedding reception. Many people have watched popular movies and television shows that showcase dance as a form of competition or entertainment. The majority of people, though, have had far less experience with dance as a fine art. Because of this limited exposure, interpreting, evaluating, and responding to dance can seem daunting. In this chapter, you will learn to evaluate and discuss dance in terms of its function, choreographic elements, and theatrical features.

Considering the Functions of Dance: Ritual, Social, Political, and Concert

When viewing dance, one of the first things to consider is what function the dance serves. Dance has four major purposes: ritual (or religious), social (or folk or ethnic), political, and concert. Our understanding of the function of a particular dance, as well as its history, can aid us in evaluating and interpreting the dance. For example, we would have difficulty evaluating an Indian temple dance and classical ballet in the same way.

The primary purpose of dance in ancient cultures was ritual. Ritual dances in many world cultures have been handed down from generation to generation just as stories and legends have been. Ritual dances generally portray or reinforce religious values and traditions and may be either literal (such as the acting out of a successful hunt) or abstract (such a series of steps, poses, and patterns with no apparent meaning). We will discuss ritual dance in more detail in Chapter 2.

Social dance is performed primarily for the entertainment of participants. While there may or may not be an audience, the entertainment value of these dances is in the performing rather than the viewing. Social dances serve a primarily recreational purpose, although another important purpose of social dance is courtship. In cultures around the world, social dance serves as a way to meet and evaluate suitable partners. While social dances may take place on special occasions, they can be differentiated from ritual dance in that they are not a central part of the special event. For example, in 21st century America we often participate in dances as part of a wedding reception. These are social dances. In a culture with a ritual wedding dance, the dance would actually be considered part of the marriage ceremony. We will discuss social dance in more detail in Chapter 3.

Political dance is almost as old as ritual dance. This type of dance was used to honor and entertain kings, pharaohs, chiefs, and emperors. In different cultures, from France to Japan to Ghana, dance was used to reinforce the power and might of the ruling class. Political dance generally includes elaborate costumes, theatrics, and a sense of propriety and decorum. In several cases, political dances evolved and developed into concert dance forms. This is due largely to the financial support or patronage of the royal courts. We will discuss political dance in more detail in Chapter 4.

Concert dance is dance with an artistic purpose. Trained dancers perform concert dance with the purpose of entertaining or engaging the audience. Concert dance is dance as a fine art and includes genres such as ballet, modern dance, and jazz dance. Chapters 5 through 7 cover various types of concert dance.

Finally, while we have discussed four specific and discrete functions of dance, it is important to remember that many forms of dance blur the lines between two or even three categories. The Spanish flamenco, for example, originated as the social dance of the Spanish gypsies. Today, audiences attend flamenco shows in theatres around the world, blurring the line between social and concert dance. BharataNatyam, a specific type of Indian classical dance, was originally performed only in Hindu temples for ritual purposes. Today, BharataNatyam is also performed in theatres for public audiences, blurring the line between ritual and concert dance. Increasingly, concert dance choreographers may use social or ritual dance influences in their concert dance choreography. Now that we have a basic understanding of the functions of dance, and how these functions can change and evolve, let us consider the elements that are used to create dance.

Considering the Choreographic Elements of Dance: Body, Time, Space, and Effort

Visual artists consider shape, form, texture, and color in their creative processes, while musicians consider harmony, rhythm, and tempo. What, then, are the artistic tools of the dance choreographer? How exactly is a dance formed? Rudolf Von Laban, a movement theorist working in the first half of the 20th century, suggested that all dances are formed by the manipulation of four elements: the body, time, space, and effort.

These four elements allow us to describe and discuss dance by answering the following four questions: Who is dancing? When do the dancers move? Where are the dancers moving? How are the dancers moving?

The Body: Who is dancing?

A dance choreographer may select dancers based on their ages, genders, training, or some combination of these. The choreographer selects dancers who will ultimately be able to convey his or her message, idea, or intention to the audience.

Number of Dancers: The number of dancers can have a significant impact on our interpretation of and response to a piece of choreography. Often a solo gives a dance a personal feel. If the dance is about struggle, we might interpret it as an individual's struggle. If the dance is about happiness, we might interpret it as an individual's happiness. A piece of choreography with two dancers generally leads us to think about some type of relationship. This might be a romantic relationship, a friendship, or a parent-child relationship. A dance performed by a large group has a very different feel. Consider two pieces of choreography by Alvin Ailey. These two dances have many similarities. How does the number of dancers performing influence your overall interpretation of the dances?

Gender of Dancers: Take a moment to close your eyes and envision a masculine movement. Now picture a feminine movement. The gender of a dancer can influence our interpretation of a dance. In the ritual and social dances of many cultures around the world, there are specific movements or even entire dances that are designed for men and those that are designed for women. In more traditional concert dance forms, such as classical ballet, we can clearly see a difference in masculine versus feminine dance movement. In recent years, though, contemporary choreographers have challenged our traditional ideas about masculinity and femininity. The subject matter of a dance might also dictate the gender of the performers.

Time: When do the dancers move?

Dance is different than visual art in that it exists only during a given time. Within each dance, the choreography determines when specific movements will take place. When to end one movement and start another is what dancers and choreographers refer to as timing. The element of time includes the following sub-headings: tempo, rhythmic patterns, and non-musical timing. In the vast majority of ritual, social, and concert dance around the world, timing is dictated by music. Quite simply, the dancers know when to move by listening to the music. We will discuss the musical components of time first, and exceptions to musical timing at the end of the section.

Tempo: Tempo, or speed, describes how slowly or quickly the dancers are moving. Often the dancers' tempo is dictated by the music. This means that the dancers move slowly to slower music and speed up their movements as the music becomes faster. Varying tempos can be used simply to make a dance more interesting, and sometimes choreographers might choose to contrast the speed of the movements with the tempo of the music with interesting results. Tempo can also be used to convey meaning, intention, or to illustrate some aspect of a particular character in a dance. Think back to *Witness* by Alvin Ailey. How does the change in tempo midway through the dance influence our interpretation of the choreographer's message?

Rhythmic Patterns: Music is divided into measures, or repeating sound patterns. Generally, the first beat of a measure is accented. This gives the movement a smooth and predictable quality. Sometimes choreographers choose to emphasize different beats; this creates syncopated rhythms. These syncopated rhythms are common in African drumming, and are consequently used more in jazz and tap dance as both of these dance forms have African roots.

Non-musical Timing: Sometimes choreographers choose to work without music. How, then, do the dancers know when to move? A dance may be timed to spoken word, such as poetry or a short story. The dancers listen for key words, phrases, or syllables to know when to move. Sometimes, too, dances are performed in silence.In these cases, the dancers may time their movements based on breath (inhalation and exhalation), on silent counts (by counting silently and consistently), or on visual cues (when dancer A moves her arm to the left, dancers B and C know to turn to the right).

Space: Where are the dancers moving?
The concept of space refers to more than just whether a dancer is performing on a stage, in a temple, or at a wedding reception. Space refers more specifically to how the dancer is using the performance area to create shapes with the body. Is the dancer using personal space (the area immediately surrounding the body) or general space (the larger performance area)? Is the movement happening on a low (crouching) or high (leaping) plane? The components of the element space include shape, level, depth/width, direction, focus, and floor patterns.

Shape: We can use the term shape to describe a very specific dance movement or to more generally describe a complete piece of choreography. Shape describes the form(s) created by the body's position in space. The dichotomous variables of shape are open/closed, symmetrical/asymmetrical, and angular/curved. An open shape extends outward from the center of the body, while a closed shape pulls the body inward. In a symmetrical shape, each side of the body is a mirror image of the other. In an asymmetrical shape, the right and left halves of the body are positioned differently. In an angular shape the joints are bent sharply, creating angles. Curved shapes are softer and rounder. A choreographer can use shape simply to add visual interest to a dance, but shape can also be used to help convey or reinforce the theme or intention of a particular piece. A dance withan overall closed, angular, and symmetrical shape might have a very robotic feel. In contrast, a dance with more open, curved, and asymmetrical shapes might appear more joyous and free. Keep in mind that shape is just one aspect of space; our overall understanding of a choreographer's intention will also be influenced by a variety of other factors.

Level: Level refers to where in the vertical plane the dancer is moving. We can describe level in terms of low (kneeling, crouching, squatting, rolling on the floor), medium (upright, neutral position), and high (leaping, being lifted, rising up with lifted arms). Just as with shape, we can discuss the level of a specific movement as well as the overall level used in a piece of choreography. Classical ballet, for example, uses primarily medium and high levels. Levels can be used to add visual interest to choreography, but they can also be used to convey or reinforce a choreographer's theme or intention. A dance about depression or inner struggle might use primarily low and medium levels, while a celebratory, joyous dance might use primarily medium and high levels.

Depth/Width: Depth and width refer to where in the horizontal and sagittal planes the dancer is moving. How far forward and back and how far right and left is the dancer moving? A choreographer may make choices about depth and width simply to add visual interest to a dance. Depth and width might also be used to convey or reinforce the choreographer's intention.

Type of Stage: A choreographer must consider the type of stage space on which the dancers will be performing. Will the audience see the dancers from only one side, or will the audience be seated on more than one side of the stage? The choreographer will want to consider the various perspectives that audience members might have, and may have to re-set or revise a dance if it was originally choreographed for one type of stage and will now be performed on another. Below are some common types of stages, but keep in mind that some dance performances may take place in converted, non-traditional spaces or even outside.

Proscenium Stage: The proscenium stage is characterized by a proscenium arch. The proscenium arch is the frame that separates the stage from the audience and forms an outline for the stage. Another characteristic of this space is the location of the audience on only one side of the stage area.

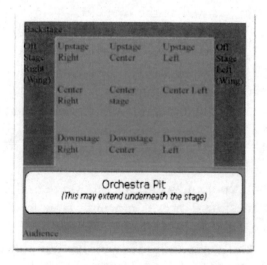

Thrust Stage: On a thrust stage, the audience is on three sides of the performance area. The dancers will be viewed by the audience from three different perspectives.

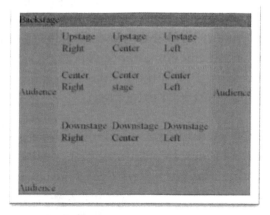

The Black Box Theatre: This stage is inside a large room that is painted black. The sets, stage, and seats can be placed or in any configuration desired by the choreographer. A black box theatre is generally a smaller, more intimate performance space.

Arena Stage or Theatre-in-the-Round: The arena stage is characterized by an area surrounded on all four sides by the audience.

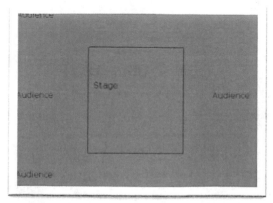

Stage Direction: Direction describes where the dancers are moving or facing. In classical ballet the dancers always face toward the audience. This tradition dates back to the royal origins of ballet. As ballet was originally performed for kings and members of the nobility, turning the back on audience members was considered rude. In other concert dance forms, including contemporary ballet, modern dance, and jazz, a choreographer might find it visually interesting for the dancers to perform some movements facing the back of the stage.

The stage directions used in dance are the same as those used in theatre. Stage right and stage left indicate the **dancer's** right and left as the dancer faces the audience. The area of the stage closest to the audience is downstage, and the area farthest from the audience is upstage. The terms upstage and downstage are derived from the medieval architectural tradition of the raked staged. During this time period, the poorest audience members stood at the bottom of the stage. In order for them to be able to see all of the action, the stage was raked, or slanted upward away from the audience. Thus, upstage and downstage literally described the high and low points on the stage. In summary, a dancer standing at the corner of the stage closest to the audience and on the audience's left would be standing downstage right.

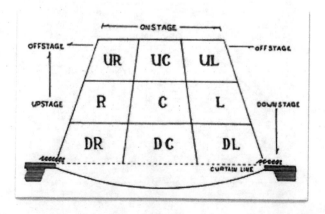

Focus: Focus describes where a dancer is projecting his or her energy. Focus is closely related to eye gaze, but is more than just eye gaze. It is a projection or concentration of energy and connects the eyes, face, and body. Because of the court origins of ballet, the focus in classical ballet is generally out towards the audience. In a dance with an introspective theme, the dancer's focus may be inward. In a passionate duet the dancers might focus exclusively on each other. In a ritual dance or praise dance the dancers might direct their focus upward.

Floor Patterns: To create floor patterns, a choreographer arranges the dancers in some recognizable, and often geometric, way. Examples of floor patterns include circles, figure eights diagonal lines, and intersecting lines. In concert dance, floor patterns can be used to create visual interest or appeal or to convey a particular feeling or intention. Many ritual dances involve a circular pattern, as this shape generally promotes the inclusion of all members of the group. In ritual dance, the infinite quality of a circle can also represent continuity and the life cycle. Many social dances use floor patterns such as circles, squares, and lines as a way to predictably structure the dance for the participants.

Effort: How are the dancers moving?
Any movement can be executed in a variety of ways. Both the amount of energy expended and the speed with which a movement is performed will influence how the movement looks. Try this simple exercise: Walk across the room purposefully, as if you are on your way to an important appointment. Now walk across the room as if you are taking a relaxing evening stroll. In both cases, the action was the same – walking. The effort was different, though, and the effect on an audience would be different as well.

Effort can be considered in terms of two variables: speed and energy level. A movement can be fast or slow, and can be performed with high energy or low energy. This gives us four possible dynamic combinations: high energy/fast, high energy/slow, low energy/fast, and low energy/slow. While it important to understand the variables that influence effort, effort is best discussed with descriptive words. While there are four possible dynamic combinations, there are thousands of descriptors for effort. Consider all of the adverbs in the English language. Was a movement performed sharply, gracefully, percussively, or languidly? These movement quality words can be used to describe individual movements or a dance as a whole.

In addition to using the elements of body, time, space, and effort to create a dance, a dance choreographer must also make choices regarding the theatrical features that he/she will use to support and enhance the dance. We will discuss these next.

Considering the Theatrical Features of Dance: Costume, Set, and Lighting

Costume: A dance costume may be as simple as a form-fitting leotard or may involve elaborate dresses, tutus, masks, or headpieces. Costumes can be used simply to create visual interest or can be used to reinforce or relate to some characteristic or mood of the dance. Costuming for dance is different than costuming for theatre in that the wearer of the costume will be required to execute a variety of athletic and technical movements. Sometimes choreographers choose extremely simple costumes so as not to detract from the movement itself. Whether or not to use an elaborate costume, and how to use the costume to reinforce the choreographic intention is ultimately up to the choreographer. The costume designer supports the choreographer by creating costumes that reinforce the vision for the piece. Keep in mind that color can be used symbolically in dance costuming just as it is in visual art and in literature. All colors have both positive and negative connotations. Red, for example, symbolizes both passion/romance and aggression/war.

Set: Dance stage sets can vary from non-existent (a bare stage), to extremely elaborate. In dance that tells a concrete story, such as classical ballet, the set becomes an important vehicle for conveying the time and place in which the action is taking place. For example, we know that Act I of *The Nutcracker* takes place at a Christmas party because of the Christmas tree, decorations, and furniture. We know that Act III of *Sleeping Beauty* takes place at the palace because of the elaborate columns and gilded staircase. In a dance that is more abstract, the choreographer may decide that a set is not necessary. In some cases, a set may be abstract, or may evoke ideas or images rather than giving a concrete sense of place and time. Finally, it is becoming more common for contemporary choreographers to use sets that also serve as props. In these cases, the dance itself could not be performed without the set.

Lighting: Lighting, like costume and set, can range from extremely simple to incredibly complex. The amount of light, the color of the light, and the way the light is used on the stage space can all impact the overall feel of a dance. Generally, a brightly lit stage will convey an open and happier mood. A dimly lit stage can convey a sense of foreboding, fear, depression, or turmoil. A spotlight on a single dancer might be used to make a dance more personal. Color symbolism, discussed earlier in reference to costuming, can also be used in lighting. As with set, lighting can sometimes become an integral part of a dance.

It is important to remember that while a choreographer always considers theatrical features and makes conscious decisions regarding costumes, set, and lighting, the impact that these features have on dances is variable. In other words, in some dances the costumes might be of primary importance. As you view more examples of concert dance, you will become more comfortable in deciding which theatrical features and elements of dance are most important or noteworthy in a given work.

Now that we have discussed the functions, choreographic elements, and theatrical features of dance, we are ready to discuss specific dance forms. In Chapter 2 we will study ritual dance from different cultures and continents. While ritual dances were not necessarily choreographed by one person and were not specifically choreographed with the intention of audience appeal, we can still discuss these dances in terms of body, time, space, and energy. We can also consider the use of theatrical effects including costumes, masks, and props. As we move into our discussion of ritual dance in Chapter 2, use the terms and concepts from this chapter to help you describe and discuss the various dance forms.

Sources Considered in this Chapter:

Ambrosio, Nora. *Learning about dance.* Dubuque, IA: Kendall Hunt, 2010.

Bradley, Karen K. *Rudolf Laban.* London; New York: Routledge, 2009.

Jonas, Gerald. *Dancing: the pleasure, power, and art of movement.* New York: Harry N. Abrams, 1992.

Kraus, Richard G. *History of the dance in art and education.* Englewood Cliffs, N.J.: Prentice-Hall, 1969.

Lihs, Harriet. *Appreciating dance.* Highstown, N.J.: Princeton Book Company, 2009.

Maletic, Vera. *Body, space, expression: the development of Rudolf Laban's movement and dance concepts.* Berlin; New York: Mouton de Gruyter, 1987.

Nadel, Myron Howard and Marc Raymond Strauss. *The dance experience.* Highstown, N.J.: Princeton Book Company, 2003.

Preston-Dunlop, Valerie and Lesley-Ann Sayers, eds. *The dynamic body in space: exploring and developing Rudolf Laban's ideas for the 21st century.* Alton, Hampshire: Dance Books, 2010.

Chapter 2

Introduction
The oldest dances in the world are ritual dances. Ritual dances were used to communicate with gods or spirits, to celebrate important rites of passage, and to pass deeply held religious and cultural beliefs from one generation to the next. In this chapter, we will discuss the history of ritual dance, the types of ritual dance, the form of ritual dance, and some specific ritual dances from around the world.

History of Ritual Dance
The oldest record of ritual dance dates back to the Paleolithic Era (30,000-10,000 B.C.). Historians' observations of ritual dance from this time period are based largely on cave paintings, which depict dancers re-enacting successful hunting expeditions. The dancers expressed, through movement and gesture, the story of the hunt. The purpose of masks and costumes, which were usually the skins of slain animals, was to make the dance as realistic as possible. Paleolithic dance is characterized by realism, as opposed to the elements of magic found in later ritual dance. The earliest purpose of this ritual dance was to tell stories or provide information.[1]

The Neolithic Era (7,000-3,000 B.C.) coincided with humanity's transition from a hunting society to an agrarian society. As humans came to increasingly rely on planting and harvesting, they learned that their ability to successfully secure food was largely outside of their control. They could plant and carefully tend their crops, but they could not control elements of nature such as rain and wind. It was during this time period that humans developed a belief in the other-worldly, or in gods and spirits. Dance became a means of communicating with these unseen forces of nature and of requesting fertile land, regulated weather, and successful harvests. These dance rituals had elements of magic to them, and were often performed in a magic circle or sacred space. Magic allowed primitive people to explain the unexplainable: weather patterns, disease, and fertility of both the land and people.[2]

As human cultures became more complex, so did their dance rituals. Originally used simply to communicate stories of the hunt, ritual dance evolved to serve a variety of purposes. These include healing, celebrating of rites of passage, and communicating with the spirit world. Ritual dance continues today, although it is difficult to find examples of purely ritual dance in Western culture. Ritual dances today exist most purely among tribal peoples living in rural areas who rely on hunting or agriculture for their existence.[3] Some characteristics of the ritual dance of the last few centuries include the use of masks and the use of a shaman or medicine man to perform dance rituals.

Masks serve several different purposes in ritual dance. Some masks, such as those of the shamans of the Eskimo, are representations of guardian spirits. The Eskimos believe that they can induce a state of trance by wearing these masks and establishing a 'link' with the spirit world. Masks can also be used as a form of protection against supernatural dangers, for example to avoid recognition by the spirits of the dead at a funeral. Masks can also form a protective barrier between the physical and spiritual realms. In these cases, wearing masks protects the performers from being completely possessed or overcome by spirits. Sometimes, too, masks are used in ritual dance to ward away evil spirits.[4]

As primitive societies became more specialized, with different members of the tribe or clan performing different tasks, the idea of a shaman or medicine man developed.

> Certain individuals were better dancers than others, were able to attain a greater degree of ecstasy, a near-perfect union with the God-given, than others. In these states, such magic-dancers were subject to visions and to prophetic utterances; these premier dancers were thus singled out for special respect and authority, and such a one was called the Shaman or medicine-man.[5]

The shaman or medicine man was responsible for performing the dance rituals and then sharing the spiritual messages, healing, and restorative powers with the tribal group.

Ritual dance continued to be important in the Ancient civilizations of Greece and Rome, although we begin to see dance performed for other purposes as well. References to dance in Ancient Greece can be found in myths, literature, sculptures, and drawings. The ritual, social, and concert functions of dance were commonly practiced. Dance was considered to be part of the total education of a well-bred Greek citizen, and was performed socially among members of the upper classes. Dance for artistic purpose, or early concert dance, can be found in the Greek chorus. Members of the chorus used movement to reinforce and respond to the spoken lines during dramatic performances. Most Greek dance, though, was tied to religious ritual. Terpsichore, goddess of the arts was often honored through dance, as was Dionysus, the god of wine.

References to dance in Ancient Egypt can found in tomb carvings and drawings. These artistic works depict elaborate funeral rituals as well as dances to honor the sun and the signs of the zodiac. There is also evidence that the first paid, professional dancers were those in Ancient Egypt. Dancers and acrobats were paid to perform in funeral rituals, but were also paid to perform at social events for the upper classes. It was considered inappropriate for a member of the Egyptian aristocracy to dance outside of a ritual event, so lower-class dancers were paid to perform. Ancient Egyptian dance is one of the oldest dance forms with a clearly defined movement vocabulary, or set system of steps and poses.

Ritual dance has declined almost directly in proportion to the decline of humans' belief in magic.[6]As humans have developed scientific and rational explanations for events such weather, the changing seasons, sickness, and infertility, the need for ritual dance has decreased.

> The process of civilization may be contradictory to the process of art and ritual. In civilization, the power of these activities is gradually displaced and abandoned as people discover cause and effect and pursue the control of nature by methods which alter the causal circumstances of their existence.[7]

Although many of the reasons for performing ritual dance have declined with the coming of civilization, many ritual dances continue to be performed as a symbol of national or tribal pride.[8] Such performances blur the lines between ritual and social dance. If ritual dance is repeatedly performed for the sheer joy of expression, it begins to take on an aesthetic function, blurring the lines between ritual and concert dance.[9]

Another reason for the decline of ritual dance is colonization and the spread of Christianity. Christian missionaries attempted to eliminate ritual dance in many areas of the world. Seldom, though were they completely successful. What happened more often is one of the following: Either the indigenous ritual dance was incorporated into the Christian church services, taking on a new religious meaning, or the function of the danced changed from a purely ritual function to more of a social function. We will see examples of this as we discuss some specific examples of ritual dance later in this chapter.

Types of Ritual Dance

While the forms, patterns, and costumes used in ritual dance vary widely from culture to culture, the same intentions or purposes are expressed repeatedly. Categorizing ritual dance based on intent will allow us to better understand the way that these dances are used among different groups.

Dances of Imitation: The ritual of the hunt is the clearest and most common dance of imitation. The dancers actually mime or act out a successful hunt with the belief that this will make the desired outcome more likely. However, even animals not hunted for food were imitated in dance ritual. These imitative rituals were performed to honor the desirable qualities, such as courage, strength, or cunning, of a particular animal.

Medicine Dances: In many cultures, medicine dances cannot be performed by all members of a tribal group but are performed only by the shaman or medicine man. Medicine dances may be performed in times of illness with the goal of restoring health to a sick individual, but medicine dances often serve as preventive care for members of the tribe or community. Medicine dances are performed to ward off evil spirits, provide protection, and prevent pain and illness. Medicine dances sometimes require the shaman to enter a trance-like state where he/she actually communicates with the spirit world. Then the messages and restorative and protective powers of the sprits can be shared with the larger community.

Commemorative Dances: Commemorative dances serve as a remembrance and celebration of special or sacred events. These dances can commemorate events that are important to the entire cultural group. These events are often astral or geological phenomenon, such as the summer solstice, the full moon, or a volcanic eruption. The Hawaiian Hula is an example of a dance that commemorates events of importance to the cultural group. Sacred hulas celebrate Pele, the goddess of the volcano, and commemorate the volcanic eruptions that created the Hawaiian Islands.

Commemorative dances can also celebrate rites of passage, or important events in an individual's life. Examples of these individual milestones include birth, the transition from boyhood to manhood or girlhood to womanhood, marriage, and death. Dances that initiate the performers into adulthood may include tests of physical and mental prowess and may last for days or weeks.

Dances of Transcendence: As we have discussed here, the power of religious belief among primitive peoples is extraordinary. It is so strong in some cases that participants believe they can actually transcend the physical realm and make contact with the spirit world. In many cases, these transcendent experiences are aided by the use of mind-altering activities or substances.

Some Native American dance rituals include the use of peyote, a cactus bud with hallucinogenic effects, and Indonesian dance rituals sometimes include the use of opiates. Lack of sleep, meditative drumming, and herbal teas may also be used to help dancers achieve a transcendent state.

Just as some dances blur the lines between ritual, social, and/or concert dance, keep in mind that ritual dances can blur the lines between the four types discussed above. For example, a medicine dance might also involve the shaman seeking a transcendent experience. A commemorative dance to celebrate initiation to adulthood might involve a young boy imitating a totem animal, blurring the lines between a commemorative dance and a dance of imitation.

Commonalities in the Form of Ritual Dance

While ritual dances vary widely from culture to culture and also vary within cultures based on the purpose or intention of the ritual, there are some generalizations that we can make about ritual dance around the world. Recognizing that these descriptions are not accurate for all ritual dances and that each ritual dance must, to some extent, be viewed in its own context, here are some common characteristics of ritual dances around the world:

Processionals: Many ritual dances begin with processions to a sacred space or altar. Egyptian funeral rituals, celebrations to honor the Greek gods, and even medieval Christian pilgrimages included processional, patterned walks or marches. A wedding party's walk down the aisle is an example of a modern day ritual procession.

Circular Patterns: Circle dances were performed by the ancient Hebrews, ancient Greeks, and by many Native American tribes. Circles are popular patterns in ritual dance because the shape is evocative of the infinite and cyclical nature of the universe. The seasons and solar/lunar phenomenon were understood by primitive people to be cyclical, with no beginning and no end. The circle was a fitting visual representation of these events. Further, the circular shape is inclusive, allowing each participant to take an equal role in the celebration.

Bent-Knee Positions: In many ritual dances the dancers' knees are bent and their bodies are tilted forward from the waist. This is a visual representation of the dancers' closeness to the earth. Unlike Western dance, which fights or defies gravity, many ritual dances give in to gravity. The dancers use primarily low and medium levels. For many indigenous tribes, the spirit world is not located in the skies or heavens. Instead, power and sustenance come from the earth. By dancing with the knees bent, the performers both draw power from the earth and give honor and respect to the earth. Agnes de Mille further suggests that the bent-knee position found in many ritual dances may have been a result of primitive man's nakedness and vulnerability, and may have been an attempt to protect vital areas.[10]

Animal-like Movements: The movements of birds, fish, and other animals were sources of inspiration for primitive peoples. Many indigenous groups believed that animals possessed souls. They further believed in reincarnation and accepted the idea that a soul could migrate between humans and animals during different lives. Just as animals appear frequently in ancient myths and legends and also in primitive drawings and carvings, animal-like movements appear frequently in ritual dance.[11]

Use of Rhythmic Timing: Ritual dances in most cultures around the world are closed tied to rhythms. Often ritual dance is accompanied by drumming, chanting, or both. Rhythmic and complex foot movements are often stressed in primitive dance, and bells may be tied to the hands or feet to further amplify these rhythms.

Ritual Dance Across the Continents
Africa: Dance has always been an important part of life in African society. Ritual dances of transcendence help people to understand and remember their role in relation to the divine. Commemorative dances of initiation contribute a sense of cultural continuity. Medicine dances ensure physical well-being. While over time some aspects of African dance have also adapted and changed, today ritual dance remains an important element in the spiritual and emotional well-being of many African cultures.[12]

The Mbende Jerusarema

The Mbende Jerusarema dance of Zimbabwe has been passed down through many generations and remains one of the most important traditional dance performances in contemporary Zimbabwe. The dance was originally performed as a protective measure. During times of imminent war, women would perform the dance for an audience of the opposing forces while the elderly men of the tribe played the drums. This allowed the warriors to scout the enemy forces and prepare for battle. Because the dance is sensual and was originally performed by women, some believe that the dance originated as a fertility ritual, but the theory of the dance as a preparation for battle is more widely accepted. In more recent times, the dance has evolved to serve a commemorative purpose and is used on ceremonial occasions.

Today the Mbende Jerusarema is performed by women and men together and is characterized by sensual, acrobatic waist-shaking and hip movements. It is these movements that made the dance unpopular amongst the Christian missionaries, who found them sexually explicit. The missionaries collaborated with the Native Commissioners, or local government, to ban Mbende Jerusarema on the grounds that the dance was a hindrance to the Christian conversion of the locals. Despite attempts to repress the dance form, it has survived and flourished.

The Mbende Jerusarema has been characterized as a dance of imitation in the sense that it imitates an animal, specifically a mouse or burrowing mole. The purpose, though, is not exclusively imitative, but is instead to use the mouse or mole as a symbol of the desirable qualities of quickness, fertility, sexuality and family.[13]

North America: Dance rituals were integrated into almost every aspect of Native American life. Dance was used to seek connections with nature and spirits, to celebrate rites of passage, to heal sickness, and to prepare for war. Today, many Native American tribes use dance rituals to protect their warriors who are members of our modern-day military forces.

The circular pattern has always been the primary formation in Native American dance, due largely to the ancient belief that everyone and everything is part of the same universe. This interconnection of man and nature is a key element of native belief systems. Although men and women sometimes share specific dances, most are male or female-only. Nearly all are accompanied by drums, and many use elaborate costumes and masks.

During the nineteenth century, the westward expansion of white settlers changed native culture forever. Pressure from the U.S. Army coupled with a drastic reduction in the size of buffalo herds drove most Plains Indians to reservations. Recognizing the discontent that this caused among the native people, and fearing that ritual dance might unite the people in uprising against the United States government, bans on ritual dancing were instituted. From the 1880's through the 1930's the United States Department of Indian Affairs banned all native dance ceremonies.

Once these bans on dancing were lifted, the function of Native American dance began to change. In the 1930's, some pow-wows became "inter-tribal," meaning that they were open for all tribes to attend, and the practice of "contesting" began. Contesting involves dance competitions that may last all weekend, taking into account how often dancers perform as well as how well they may perform the dances. What once were purely sacred dances are now performed in a social context. Today Native American pow-wows may be open to the public, adding an element of concert dance as well. Native American culture has shown itself to be incredibly adaptable, both retaining ancient heritage and advancing with the times.[14]

The Apache Mountain Spirit Dance

One of the most important holy beings for Apaches is White-Painted Woman. Her sons, Killer of Enemies and Child Born of Water, are the Mountain Spirits. These spirits triumphed over all the evils of the world, making it safe for humans. The Mountain Spirits ensure the well-being of the people by protecting them from both diseases and enemies. The Mountain Spirit Dancers, also called Crown Dancers or Gan dancers, "become" these sacred beings. The dancers become a physical manifestation of the spiritual world, and share the blessings of the spirits with the tribe.

The dance is traditionally performed by four dancers and a sacred clown*. Their faces are covered with buckskin hoods and their heads are crowned with wooden slat headdresses. The dancers hold wooden swords and are accompanied by drumming. The dance is traditionally performed as part of a girl's initiation ceremony, which lasts for four days, but may be performed on other occasions as well. [15]

> *The sacred clown is a common convention in Native American ritual dance. The clown ridicules both himself and others, including the shaman and tribal elders. The dual nature of reality is an important aspect of Native American culture and beliefs, so serious ritual and humor can easily exist side by side.

South America: In the late 15th and early 16th centuries, explorers from Spain and Portugal landed on the South American continent and encountered cultures unknown to Europeans. A few of the Europeans wrote about the music and dance practices they observed during ritual festivals among the local populations. Based on these writings, pre-Catholic South American ritual dance appears to have many similarities to

Native American dance. The creation story was a common theme in indigenous ritual dance, and nature gods and animal spirits were honored or represented through dance. The great civilizations of the Aztec and the Inca organized time according to complex ritual calendars, and dance was an important part of this communal ritual life.

The dances of the Aztec were precisely structured and executed. Priests and elders trained young people in the movements of the ritual dances and organized the ceremonies into massive arrangements of dancers who moved in symbolic geometric patterns. In some ceremonies dancers moved in columns to represent revolving astral bodies in their circuits; in others they represented planters working in the fields.[16]

Danza de Tijeras

Performed in the central and southern highlands of Peru, La Danza de Tijeras, or the Scissors Dance, is a traditional event that tests the physical and spiritual strength of the participants. While Westerners often interpret La Danza de Tijeras as a physical competition between two men, the people of the Andes view this dance is a sacred ritual. The dancers, called danzaq, perform difficult stunts and leaps, accompanied by music from a violin, a harp and the sound of the scissors they hold in their hands.

The origin of the Danza de Tijeras is shrouded in mystery, but some anthropologists believe that it appeared in 1524, during the rebellion against Spanish colonial rule. In reaction to forced Christian conversion, the prophets of the Andes foretold the end of the world for Europeans and those Andean people who adopted Christianity as their faith. From this prophecy were born elaborate rituals, most importantly the furious dancing of La Danza de Tijeras. The dancers dance as if possessed by the spirits who were angered at the Andean peoples' abandonment of the indigenous religion. When the Andean religion was suppressed and its temples destroyed, the natives believed that the gods took refuge in the bodies of their believers. The gods were said to possess the bodies of indigenous young men, allowing them to perform a wild dance invoking the return of the Old Gods.

Today the tradition of the Scissors Dance is kept alive by the Andean people. The dance is competitive, requiring the dancers to prove their spiritual superiority. The performers go through a series of challenges and display an extraordinary ability to withstand pain in order to beat their opponents.[17]

Australia: For the Native Australians, the Aboriginal people, the land is sacred. Knowledge of sacred sites is learned through a process of initiation which includes the learning of Aboriginal law. These laws are not public knowledge, and the existence of many sacred sites might not be broadcast to the wider world unless they are threatened. Many dance rituals take place in these sacred places. Aboriginal ceremonies, known as corroborees, are dramatic representations of the mythical history of the tribe. These ceremonies have many functions and take many forms.

Dreamtime Dances
The Aborigines believe that during creation, a time known as the Dreamtime, their ancestors' spirits came to the earth in human form and created the animals, plants, rocks and other features of the land. Once these ancestor spirits created the world, they themselves changed into trees, stars, rocks, watering holes or other natural objects. Because the ancestors did not disappear at the end of the Dreamtime, but remained in these sacred sites, the Dreaming is never-ending, providing a link between the past and the present, the people and the land. Much of Australia's native ritual dance focuses on re-enacting this Dreamtime, or creation

myth. Aborigines also believe that they can use dance rituals to communicate with the spirits of their ancestors.[18]

Europe: - Most European ritual dances have their roots in pre-Christian times. The indigenous pagan religions of Europe were polytheistic, and ritual dances likely resembled the Greek dance rituals that honored different gods and goddesses. Certain ritual dances were performed at particular times of the year.

As the Catholic Church came to power in Europe, ritual dance was banned. The Catholic Church clearly divided the physical world from the spiritual world. Dance, because it was of the body, was seen as immoral and even evil. Despite bans on dancing, though, ritual dances were difficult to suppress. In order to "manage" this pagan dancing, some seasonal rituals were given new names and purposes that coincided with events on the Church calendar. In other words, what was once a harvest ritual was reassigned to be the dance of a particular saint's feast day. Many of these dances further evolved into the social/ethnic dances of Europe.

The Calus Dance
The Calus is a traditional Romanian folk dance that originally derives from Southern Romania. The dancers are called "calusari," which translates to "horse men". The dance is thought to be derived from a pre-Christian fertility ritual and is said to bring luck, health and happiness to the villages in which it is performed. The calusari team is composed of an odd number of men, regardless of age or marital status. They wear white trousers and white tunics, with brightly colored ribbons tied to their hats. Bells are attached to their ankles, and the dancers use sticks, which they hold upright during the dancing.[19]

*India:*Indian dance dates back to between 2300 and 1700 B.C. The Hindu religion honors Shiva, the god of creation and destruction, as the Lord of the Dance. He is often pictured standing on one leg, as if dancing the world into existence. Other gods associated with the act of dancing are Vishnu and Krishna.

Until the 20th Century, Indian temple dance was performed by devadasi, or young female devotees who lived in the temple and were dedicated to the service of a particular god. In the 20th Century concerns with human rights and women's rights led to the devadasi tradition being outlawed. This ban threatened the continuation of Indian temple dance, but the dance tradition has been continued by those interested in preserving India's cultural heritage. Members of the Brahmin class in India as well as many Westerners of Indian descent have established schools to teach Indian ritual dance.

Indian temple dance is primarily performed by women. It does vary extensively from region to region, with some temple dances using male performers. Indian dance forms place heavy emphasis on the hand gestures, or mudras, and facial expressions that are used to tell the stories of the gods. There are specific facial expressions and gestures that convey certain moods or emotions; these expressions have different versions for male and female characters.

Bharata Natyam

Bharata Natyam honors the god Krishna. The single female dancer performs two roles: that of Krishna and that of his human lover. The dance literally expresses the blissful relationship between the two lovers, but can be interpreted in a larger sense as an expression of the love of the god for humanity. The dance celebrates the entire universe through the celebration of the beauty of the physical body.

Today, Bharata Natyam is almost as likely to be seen in a recital hall as it is to be seen in a temple. Like many dance forms that originally served a purely ritual function, Bharata Natyam now serves a concert function as well. Almost all of the ritual dance forms discussed in this chapter are now blended to serve social and/or concert functions, too. In the next chapter, we will discuss social dance, or dance as a participatory activity.

Endnotes

1. Richard Kraus, *History of the Dance in Art and Education* (Englewood Cliffs, N.J.: Prentice-Hall, 1969), p. 17.

2. Richard Kraus, *History of the Dance in Art and Education* (Englewood Cliffs, N.J.: Prentice-Hall, 1969), p. 18.

3. Richard Kraus, *History of the Dance in Art and Education* (Englewood Cliffs, N.J.: Prentice-Hall, 1969), p. 15.

4. Henry Pernet, *Ritual Masks – Deceptions and Revelations* (Columbia, S.C.: University of South Carolina Press, 1992), p. 10.

5. Ted Shawn, *Dance We Must* (London: Dennis Dobson Ltd., 1946) p.55.

6. Richard Kraus, *History of the Dance in Art and Education* (Englewood Cliffs, N.J.: Prentice-Hall, 1969), p. 25.

7. Jamake Highwater, *Dance: Rituals of Experience* (Pennington, N.J.: Priceton Book Company, 1978), p. 30.

8. Richard Kraus, *History of the Dance in Art and Education* (Englewood Cliffs, N.J.: Prentice-Hall, 1969), p. 25.

9. Jamake Highwater, *Dance: Rituals of Experience* (Pennington, N.J.: Priceton Book Company, 1978), p. 29.

10. Agnes de Mille, *The Book of the Dance* (New York: Golden Press, 1963), p. 32-33.

11. Richard Kraus, *History of the Dance in Art and Education* (Englewood Cliffs, N.J.: Prentice-Hall, 1969), p. 18-19.

12. Doris Green, "Traditional Dance in Africa" in *African Dance*, Kariamu Welsh Asante ed. (Trenton, N.J.: Africa World Press, 1996), p. 13

13. Kariamu Welsh Asante, "The Jerusarema Dance of Zimbabwe," <u>Journal of Black Studies</u> 1985, Vol. 15, No. 4, p. 381-403.

14. Gerald Jonas, *Dancing: The Pleasure, Power, and Art of Movement* (New York: Harry N. Abrams, Inc., 1992), p. 28.

15. Jamake Highwater, *Ritual of the Wind* (New York: Viking Press, 1977), p. 82-86.

16. "Latin American dance." *Encyclopædia Britannica. Encyclopædia Britannica Online.* 17. Encyclopædia Britannica Inc., 2012. Web. 25 Apr. 2012. http://www.britannica.com/EBchecked/topic/1481999/Latin-American-dance.

17. "Danzantes De Tijeras YawarChicchiDe Huancavelica - Peru." Web.25 Apr. 2012 http://www.danzadelastijeras.org. Translated by Susan Marconyak.

18. "Aboriginal Australia Art and Culture Center- Alice Springs." Web.29Apr. 2012 http://www.aboriginalart.com.au/didgeridoo/ceremony.html.

19. "Calusari Dance History and Background." Web.30Apr.2012 http://www.dunav.org.il/dance_research/romania_calusari.html.

20. Gerald Jonas, *Dancing: The Pleasure, Power, and Art of Movement* (New York: HarryN. Abrams, Inc., 1992), p. 36.

Chapter 3

Introduction

Martin Stokes states that, "Music is socially meaningful not entirely but largely because it provides means by which people recognize identities and places, and the boundaries which separate them."[1] The same is true of social dance. Social dances are a source of cultural identity. They are reflections of the societies in which they originate. While social dance is performed primarily for the entertainment of the participants, and there may or may not be an audience, theses dances can convey important cultural beliefs and traditions. A very conservative culture, for example, may not permit men and women to dance together. As social and cultural values change over time, these changes are reflected in social dance. For example, the popular social dance forms of America in 1950 looked very different from the popular social dances of today.

The two most common types of social dance today are courtship dances, which serve as a way to meet and evaluate suitable partners, and communal dances, which serve to build a sense of community between members of a group. Social dance is one way that a society passes important social skills from one generation to the next. Through dance, young people learn society's expectations of them. They also learn many gender-specific behaviors, the appropriate ways for males and females to behave. This chapter will have two primary purposes - to trace the evolution of social dance in the United States and to compare and contrast social dance in several different world cultures.

History of Social Dance in the United States

The earliest roots of American social dance are in the dance forms of medieval Europe (roughly 400-1400 B.C.). Although social dancing was condemned by the Catholic Church during this time period, bans on dancing were largely ignored. In the late Middle Ages, members of the nobility began to hire dancing masters to teach the latest court dances. The basis of these court dances was often the wilder, more unrestrained dances of the European peasants. These dances were refined and codified; dancing masters ensured that dances were performed correctly. Rather than the leaps, hops, and kicks of the peasant dances, the dances of the nobles consisted of walking or gliding steps. For the first time there was a right way and a wrong way to perform social dance.[2]

The social dances of the thirteenth to fifteenth centuries (1200-1400 A.D.) were processional-type dances with relatively simple steps. Courtship dances were often line dances, which allowed the participants to interact with more than one partner during the dance as the lines rotated and partners switched. Because these dances were technically simplistic, participants were able to engage in conversation or flirtation as they came into contact with different partners for a few steps or turns. While some later medieval social dances were couple dances, the contact between partners was limited to the holding of one hand.[3]

Social dancing became increasingly popular during the Renaissance period (1400-1600 A.D.). Dance was considered to be a part of the comprehensive education of members of the nobility, and Renaissance court dance was viewed as a discipline to be studied rather than merely a physical exercise to be performed. With the advent of the printed word, dance manuals were printed and circulated; this shows clearly the importance of social dance during this time period. Popular social dances during this time period included slow, stately dances such as the bassedanze, pavane, and allemande, as well as more spirited, energetic dances such as the galliard, courante, and volta. Regardless of the specific steps involved, Renaissance dance required prior instruction and rehearsal with a dancing master. The dances were designed to appear effortless; it was undesirable for members of the nobility to show signs of physical exertion.[4]

Beginning in the seventeenth century, the waltz forever changed Western social dance. During the medieval and Renaissance time periods, marriages among members of the nobility were often arranged in order to achieve political and economic goals. The social dances of these time periods were formal and dignified. Couple dancing was generally performed at arms' length with minimal body contact. Thus the waltz, at its inception, was considered quite shocking and even scandalous. The close embrace required for the waltz also paralleled changing social views. Just as the waltz set performers free from the restricted movements and set poses of earlier court dances, the decline of the aristocracy and the rise of a powerful middle class promoted personal freedom and independence, particularly in the selection of a marriage partner.[5]

In England and the United States, the late eighteenth and nineteenth centuries witnessed a blend between the structured group dances of the rural countryside and the romantic couple dances of the upper classes. Often these dances involved "calling," or announcing the movements just before they happened. These dances, including contra dances, cotillions, and square dances, often involved flirtation and partner-swapping.[6] In addition to the development of these new blended dance forms, the waltz continued to evolve.

The waltz of the early 1800's was far more complex than the waltz of the twentieth century. The man did not lead the dance, as the steps were predetermined and rehearsed. As the waltz generalized from the nobility to the members of the middle class, though, fewer people had the benefit of formal dance lessons from a trained instructor. The steps of the dance became simplified, and this lack of formal training created the need for one partner to lead the dance. The role fell, without question, to the male.[7]

The waltz remained the most popular and prevalent social dance form among mainstream, middle-class Americans until the early 1950's. Consider the structure of the waltz: it is a couple, rather than communal, dance; the male traditionally asks the female to dance; the male leads the dance; the dance is formal and structured and there is a right way and wrong way to perform it. Now consider the social structure of middle-class America in 1950. What did a family look like? Who made the decisions? How did people socialize? How does the waltz reflect the cultural values and norms of mid-twentieth century America?

The rock-and-roll revolution of the 1950s and 60s corresponded with a social and cultural revolution in America. Largely due to the influence of Elvis Presley, popular dance in the 1950s increasingly involved movements of the hips and pelvis. Sexuality became much more evident in social dance. Further, as African-American music, including jazz and rhythm and blues, began to influence mainstream popular culture music, so did African-American dance. Dance forms such as the Charleston, Lindy Hop, and Fox Trot originated in the African-American community but became popular with all Americans during the 1950s.[8] These dances set the stage for the more independent dance styles of the 1960s and 70s because, while they required a partner, the dancers would break free from the partner for certain segments of the dance.

The dance that changed social dance forever, though, was the Twist. Popularized in the early 1960s, the Twist extended the independence and freedom of the Lindy Hop and allowed partners to move completely independently of one another. With no one to lead or follow, each person was free to pursue individual expression on the dance floor. This independent style of dance remained popular through the disco era of the 1970s and continues to be popular today. Consider the social and cultural values of present-day America. What has changed since 1950? How are these changes reflected in social dance?

Now that we have traced the evolution of social dance in the United States, we will consider the social dances of two different cultural groups. Just as social dances vary across time periods, so too do they vary across cultures. Based on your prior knowledge, how might you expect Hasidic Jewish social dance to compare to the social dances of Latin America? Make some predictions about possible similarities and differences.

Social Dance in Different World Cultures
Social Dance in Hasidic Jewish Culture:
Hasidic Judaism is a movement within Orthodox Judaism. Beginning as a grassroots religious revitalization movement, it originated in Eastern Europe in the eighteenth century, at a time when Jews were experiencing great persecution. The Hasidic movement started among the unlearned, lower classes and allowed practitioners to celebrate and experience God through the activities of daily life rather than through extensive reading and study. Fundamentally, the Hasidic religious movement was based on a less academic and more personal and emotional religious experience. The largest Hasidic groups today are located in Israel and the United States, with approximately 165,000 Hasidim living in New York City.[9]

The Hasidic way of life is highly regimented and separated from the outside world. The culture's communal orientation is visible even to outsiders. Children attend separate schools, community members use separate stores and contractors, and Hasidic neighborhoods in some cities are even demarcated by an eyruv, a wire strung high above the streets. The eyruv outlines the boundaries of the community, visually reinforcing the importance of the group.[9]

In the patriarchal Hasidic culture, men and women have very different roles and daily experiences. Women are charged with a religious obligation to raise children, while men are obligated to study the Torah and to attend daily prayer services.[10] The religious ideal for both men and women, though, is to live a life in which every moment reflects an awareness of God.

Just as the daily lives of the Hasidim are regulated by gender, so too are religious services. During prayer services in Orthodox synagogues, seating is almost always separate. A mechitzah, or cloth screen, is used to divide the men and women, and often to block the view from one section to the other, though mechitzah heights and opacity vary by synagogue.[9]

Because the Hasidim believe that God can be honored through everyday activities, and because they consider dance to be an integral part of life, social dance is permitted. Just as daily life and religious observations are gender-separate for Hasidic Jews, so too are social dances.[11]

At Hasidic weddings and bar/bat mitzvahs, seating at the ceremony and often the reception is separate, sometimes with a mechitzah or sometimes in a separate room. Social dance at these wedding receptions can be surprisingly wild, frenzied, and modern, occasionally including break-dancing or movements from current music videos. The guests use social dance to make the couple happy and joyful as they begin their new life together. Women dance on their side of the partition, and men dance on theirs. These social dances serve a communal rather than a courtship function.

Social Dance in Latin America (Rumba):

Unlike the communal function of Hasidic dance, the rumba serves a courtship function. The rumba is the oldest Latin social dance, and its name comes from the Spanish verb "rumbear," which means "to go to a party." As you might expect, the dance emphasizes fun and flirtation between genders. The dance movements of the rumba have their roots in African dance and were brought to Cuba by African slaves. The original rumba was performed to the syncopated rhythms of drums, guitars, maracas and claves, although today rumba music may include pianos and flutes.[12]

The original version of the rumba was very sexual by European standards, with prominent hip movements and a quick tempo. The dance movements are actually based on the mating movements of animals, specifically hens and roosters.[13] Throughout the dance, the male displays a sexually aggressive attitude, while the female plays a more coy or defensive role. These roles correspond with the Latin American cultural concept of machismo. Machismo is a general term that refers to manhood, courage, honor and dignity, keeping one's word, and protecting one's name. It also includes a distinction between appropriate roles for the males and females and reinforces the belief that males enjoy rights and privileges denied to females.[14]

At its inception, the rumba was performed on the streets and was very popular among the lower classes, including slaves and laborers. Because it was a dance of the lower classes, the rumba was not bound by the rules and propriety of upper class social dances, such as the waltz. Eventually, though, the sensuous nature of the dance sparked the curiosity and interest of the upper classes, and the Cuban government banned the dance. What was permissible on the streets of the slums was not acceptable for members of the upper class. Just like many other bans on dancing, this ruling was largely ignored for many years. In 1925, though, Cuban President Machado began enforcing the ban on rumba because he found the dance to be a disgrace to the reputation of the Cuban upper class. The result of this ban was a toned down version of the original rumba, a version with a slower tempo and less sensual movements. This new rumba was accepted as a ballroom social dance, and became popular in the United States by the 1920's.[15]

Summary:
Consider the similarities and differences between Hasidic dance and Latin American dance. What do the differences in these two dance forms tell us about the differences in these two cultures? Why does communal social dance look different from courtship dance? How do both of these dance forms indicate the appropriate roles for men and women in the culture? What does our social dance in the United States today say about appropriate roles for men and women? Remember that social dances reflect the societies in which they are created. As cultures evolve over time, so too do their social dances.

Endnotes

1. Martin Stokes (ed.), Introduction to *Ethnicity, Identity, and Music* (London: Berg Publishers, 1997), p. 5.

2. Carol McD. Wallace, Don McDonagh, Jean L. Druesedow, Laurence Libin, and Constance   Old, *Dance: A Very Social History* (New York: The Metropolitan Museum of Art, 1986), p. 58-59.

3. Gerald Jonas, *Dancing: The Pleasure, Power, and Art of Movement* (New York: Harry N. Abrams, Inc., 1992), p. 121.

4. Carol McD. Wallace, Don McDonagh, Jean L. Druesedow, Laurence Libin, and Constance   Old, *Dance: A Very Social History* (New York: The Metropolitan Museum of Art, 1986), p. 64-66.

5. Carol McD. Wallace, Don McDonagh, Jean L. Druesedow, Laurence Libin, and Constance   Old, *Dance: A Very Social History* (New York: The Metropolitan Museum of Art, 1986), p. 68.

6. Jane A. Harris, Anne M. Pittman, and Marlys S. Waller, *Dance A While* (New York: Macmillan, 1994), p. 57-58.

7. Gerald Jonas, *Dancing: The Pleasure, Power, and Art of Movement* (New York: Harry N. Abrams, Inc., 1992), p. 125-126.

8. Beverly H. Yerrington and Tressie A. Outland, *Social Dance* (Palo Alto, California: National Press, 1961), p. 12

9. "A Life Apart: Hasidism in America."
Web.23July2012 http://www.pbs.org/alifeapart/intro.html

10. Jerome R. Mintz, *Legends of the Hasidim* (Chicago: University of Chicago Press, 1968), p. 82-88.

11. Judith BrinIngber (ed.), *Seeing Israeli and Jewish Dance* (Detroit: Wayne State University Press, 2011), p. 240.

12. Yvonne Dabiel, *Caribbean and Atlantic Diaspora Dance* (Chicago: University of Illinois Press, 2011), p. 90-91.

13. Beverly H. Yerrington and Tressie A. Outland, *Social Dance* (Palo Alto, California: National Press, 1961), p. 12

14. Rafael L. Ramirez, *What It Means to be a Man: Reflections on Puerto Rican Masculinity* (New Brunswick, N.J.: Rutgers University Press, 1999) p. 8-9.

15. Yvonne Dabiel, *Caribbean and Atlantic Diaspora Dance* (Chicago: University of Illinois Press, 2011), p. 102-104

Chapter 4

Introduction

Political dance may be as old as ritual dance. This type of dance was used to honor and entertain kings, pharaohs, chiefs, and emperors and to reinforce the power and might of the ruling class. In many cultures, rulers were considered descendents of the gods or even gods themselves. For this reason, there are often many similarities between ritual and political dance.

The art of dance lends itself to political purpose for two important reasons. Throughout human history and across world cultures, the ruling class has sought ways to define itself as separate from the common people. From elaborate royal portraits to grand architectural design, the arts have often served this purpose. Dance and theatrics provide a rich visual display of the power and wealth of kings and emperors. Political dance generally includes elaborate costumes, intricate staging or special effects, and a sense of propriety and decorum.

The other reason that dance and politics have been joined in many cultures is a financial one. Dance, like all of the arts, needs patronage. The financial support ofthe royal courts allowed dance, the youngest of the performing arts, to develop. In Ancient Egypt, the first professional dancers were hired by the pharaoh and by the royal houses of the aristocracy to entertain on feast days. Just as Renaissance courtiers hired painters to create portraits, they also employed dancing masters to develop and teach popular social dances. Without the support of the nobility, dance may have never evolved into a concert art form.

Political dances from around the world have several commonalities. There is often a sense of spectacle which may include elaborate costuming, staging, and theatrics. Political dance is generally processional and very staid, or formal. As Gerald Jonas states, "Court dances, like other court arts from painting to architecture, tend to be conservative in the literal sense; they conserve attitudes about life that were deemed essential to the society in the past."[1] In many political dances, the dancers' places in line are related to their rankings within the court. Regardless of whether the ruler is a participant or an observer in the dance, those who stand closest to him are his most trusted advisors. Finally, political dance generally involves an emotionless, mask-like face. Just as it is considered undesirable for a ruler to make rash emotional displays, showing such emotion during dance is considered unseemly.

While there are many similarities between political dance forms across cultures and across centuries, there are differences as well. We will next consider Bugaku, the political dance of ancient Japan, and the court dances of 17th century France during the reign of Louis XIV. While different in many ways, both of these dance forms exemplify the characteristics of political dance discussed above.

Bugaku

Bugaku refers to a group of ceremonial dances that are performed both in temples and at the Imperial court of Japan. The dances were originally adopted from China and Korea in the seventh and eighth centuries and were further refined during the next three centuries. Early Bugaku (from the eighth to eleventh centuries) was a theatrical art form that allowed for a high degree of creative freedom. Over time, though, Bugaku became a lofty, highly stylized dance form that reinforced ceremonial decorum and court etiquette.[2]

The first Japanese school of music and dance was founded at the Imperial court in 701 and was supervised by Imperial officials. Native performers as well as Chinese and Korean immigrants were recruited to perform Bugaku in the Imperial court. During the Heian period (794–1192), Bugaku became more highly stylized, and the dances became a pursuit of the courtiers at the Imperial palace. "In the glorious Heian period, when court culture blossomed in Kyoto as it was never to flower again, it was one of the indispensible requirements of a nobleman to master dance and music."[3] Courtiers choreographed their own dances, which they themselves also sometimes performed. Later, when the Imperial court lost its wealth and could not afford dance groups, temples began to maintain the tradition. Today the Imperial household has an institution that is responsible for continuing Bugaku. Occasionally performances are also staged at temples and important scenic spots, as well as on public stages, removed from their court context.

While ancient Bugaku claims an extensive repertory, today there remain about 50 Bugaku works.[4] The Bugaku repertoire is divided into two basic groups, that of the "dances of the left" (*samai* or *sabu*), which were adopted from China, and that of the "dances of the right" (*umai* or *ubu*), which originally came from Korea. The two groups are differentiated by their accompanying music and costuming. In the dances derived from China the color scheme of the richly embroidered court costumes focuses on red, whereas in the dances derived from Korea the predominant color is green.[5] Many of the Bugaku dances use wooden masks. This is the case particularly with demonic characters, since any kind of facial expression in the court context is regarded as vulgar. Masks are often used to portray powerful characters.[6]

Bugaku is traditionally performed on a raised platform measuring seven by seven meters.[7] In the introductory portion of the dance, the dancers slowly appear on the stage. The tempo of the music gradually gets faster, while the dancers begin their extremely slow, solemn, minimalistic movements. Repetition and a deliberately slow tempo are the hallmarks of Bugaku. As for subject matter, some of the dances may originally have had a narrative content, such as the battle of an Indian king with an invisible opponent, the reenactment of a sporting event, or even some more comic elements such as parody. Generally, though, the ancient narrative content has been replaced by the increasing emphasis on ceremonial elegance prevalent at the Heian court.[8] Today many Bugaku dances are completely abstract. While the great works of Bugaku last up to two hours, the dances most often performed today last approximately twenty minutes.[9]

Today, Bugaku and its accompanying music, Gagaku, are passed down from generation to generation of palace servants via an oral tradition. The most talented boys from each generation are trained as performers beginning as early as age five. Only those born or adopted into a Bugaku family can perform these dances. While Bugaku was maintained as a palace secret until after World War II, in 1955 the Japanese court musicians and dancers were declared Important Intangible Government Properties, or "living national treasures."[10]

French Court Dance
The earliest precursors to the political dance of the French court were the lavish entertainments presented in the courts of fifteenth-century Renaissance Italy. These elaborate spectacles, which united painting, poetry, music, and dancing, took place in large halls that were used also for banquets and balls. Although these spectacles required an enormous amount of time, effort, and money to coordinate, many were performed a single time. The dancers who participated in these court spectacles were courtiers themselves. Performing was both a sign of their own social status and a way to show allegiance to the king, and

dancing was considered an important part of the education and training of members of the nobility.

The elaborate court spectacles of the Renaissance traveled from Italy to France with Catherine de Medici when she married Henry II. In France, the elaborate spectacles, or *ballets de cour*, became tools of political power. They were used to celebrate important political events including births, coronations, treaties, and marriages. Further, they served as important displays of the power and wealth of the king.[11]

Catherine de Medici set the new standard for court spectacle when she commissioned *Le Ballet Comique de la Reine* (The Queen's Ballet Comedy) in 1581. The first ballet for which a complete choreographic score survived, it was performed in Paris to celebrate the royal wedding of Catherine's son, the future King Henry III to the future Queen Louise. Staged by Balthazar de Beaujoyeux, a violinist and dancing master at the court of Queen Catherine de Medici, it was danced by aristocratic amateurs in a hall with the royal family seated on a dais at one end and spectators in galleries on three sides. Since much of the audience saw the ballet from above, the choreography emphasized the elaborate floor patterns created by lines and groups of dancers. Elaborate special effects, poetry, mime, acrobatics, and songs accompanied the dances during the four and a half hour performance.[12]

Most French court ballets consisted of dance scenes linked by a minimum of plot. Because they were designed principally for the entertainment of the aristocracy, rich costumes, scenery, and elaborate stage effects were emphasized. The proscenium stage was first adopted in France in the mid-1600s, and professional dancers made their first appearance, although they were not permitted to dance in the grand ballet that concluded the performance; this was still reserved for the king and courtiers.

Political dance in France reached its peak during the reign (1643-1715) of Louis XIV, whose title the Sun King was derived from a role he danced in the Le Ballet de la Nuit. In this ballet, Louis XIV played Apollo, the sun god; he was circled by masked courtiers who represented the planets revolving around the sun.[13] Louis used ballet and his carefully selected roles to reinforce the idea that he ruled by divine right and that he alone was the center of power in France. "In the person of Louis we find a highly appropriate expression of the process by which royal dynasties had come about, had made themselves absolute and adopted a divine sanction."[14]

At his palace in Versailles, Louis housed one thousand titled members of the nobility. Louis the XIV was expected to entertain this large entourage, and he did so primarily with dance. When Louis was at residence at Versailles during peacetime, he hosted two or three balls a week. These balls were not merely opportunities for social dancing, but were political events where careers and fortunes were made and lost. They further served to keep the nobles busy; Louis believed that the more time they spent mastering dances, the less time they would have to plot against him. The balls always opened with a double-file line dance, the branle. Men lined up behind the King, women behind the Queen. Nobles were arranged in line by rank, with the most important standing closest to the King and Queen. Following the branle, couples dancing began with the King and Queen. Only one couple danced at a time, so there was ample opportunity for both political discussion and the critique of dance technique. Daily dancing lessons were considered time well spent for courtiers, as dance was clearly a way to move up the political ladder.[15] If the role of dance in French politics seems strange to us in today, consider for a moment the role that golf sometimes plays in conducting important business deals or transactions. In certain instances, might someone today consider taking golf lessons as a way to get ahead in business?

In addition to using dance politically, Louis the XIV is known as a great patron of dance. He established schools for dancing, hired dancing masters, and supported the emergence of ballet as a concert art form. Truly, the roots of the ballet we know today are in the French court of Louis XIV. We will discuss the development of ballet in more detail in Chapter 5.

Endnotes

1. Gerald Jonas, *Dancing: The Pleasure, Power, and Art of Movement* (New York: Harry N. Abrams, Inc., 1992), p. 107.

2. Benito Ortolani, *The Japanese Theatre* (New Jersey: Princeton University Press, 1990), p. 39.

3. Thomas Immoos, *Japanese Theatre* (New York: Rizzoli International, 1974), p. 50

4. Thomas Immoos, *Japanese Theatre* (New York: Rizzoli International, 1974), p. 50

5. Yoshinobu Inoura and Toshio Kawatake, *The Traditional Theater of Japan* (New York: John Weatherhill, Inc., 1981), p. 36.

6. Benito Ortolani, *The Japanese Theatre* (New Jersey: Princeton University Press, 1990), p. 49.

7. Thomas Immoos, *Japanese Theatre* (New York: Rizzoli International, 1974), p. 51.

8. Benito Ortolani, *The Japanese Theatre* (New Jersey: Princeton University Press, 1990), p. 45.

9. Thomas Immoos, *Japanese Theatre* (New York: Rizzoli International, 1974), p. 50

10. Gerald Jonas, *Dancing: The Pleasure, Power, and Art of Movement* (New York: Harry N. Abrams, Inc., 1992), p. 103.

11. Jenifer Nevile, ed., *Dance, Spectacle, and the Body Politick* (Indianapolis: Indiana University Press, 2008), p. 99.

12. Jenifer Nevile, ed., *Dance, Spectacle, and the Body Politick* (Indianapolis: Indiana University Press, 2008), p. 105.

13. Wendy Hilton, *Dance and Music of Court and Theater* (Stuyvesant, NY: Pendragon Press, 1997), p. 7.

14. Laurence Bradford Packard, *The Age of Louis XIV* (New York: Henry Holt and Company, 1929), p. 16.

15. Wendy Hilton, *Dance and Music of Court and Theater* (Stuyvesant, NY: Pendragon Press, 1997), p. 11.

Chapter 5

Ballet

In Chapter 4 we considered dance in the French court of Louis XIV. The roots of ballet are to be found in this French court dance and, further back, in the social dances of the Renaissance. But how did these social and political dance forms evolve into a concert art form? Remember that concert dance is performed by trained professionals for an audience. When did European dance become a professional endeavor? When did members of the aristocracy become audience members rather than participants? In order to answer these questions we must look further at Louis XIV, considered by many to be the father of ballet.

Early Ballet

In addition to using dance as a political instrument, Louis XIV was also interested in dance as a concert art form. Louis performed in concert dance himself, often appearing as Apollo the Sun God, but his most important contribution to dance was the establishment and patronage of a school for ballet. Ballet as the art form we know today was born in 1661 when Louis XIV established the Royal Academy of Dance, the world's first ballet school. The Royal Academy of Dance was attended only by men, as any form of acting was considered disgraceful for women. Pierre Beauchamps became the ballet master of the Royal Academy. It is Beauchamps who is credited with standardizing the five positions of the feet in ballet.

In 1669 Louis XIV, established another academy, the Royal

Academy of Music, run by composer Jean Baptiste Lully. Lully soon established a dance academy within the Royal Academy of Music, and by 1672 these institutions were known as the Paris Opera and the Paris Opera Ballet. The Paris Opera Ballet remains the world's oldest continuously running ballet company. Lully's seriousness towards the study of dance led to the development of professional dancers as opposed to courtiers who could dance. Prior to 1681 ballet was performed almost exclusively by men. In 1681 women were admitted as performers in the Paris Opera Ballet. That same year Lully staged *Le Triomphe de l'Amour*, featuring Mademoiselle de Lafontaine. Lafontaine was quickly hailed as the "Queen of Dance." During this early ballet period men continued to outshine women as performers, due largely to the heavy, burdensome costumes required for female dancers. Relatively quickly, though, women became the stars of the Romantic ballet.

Romantic Ballet (1800-1850)

In the early nineteenth century, innovations in costumes and lighting, as well as political changes in France led to the rise of the Romantic period in ballet. Prior to this time period, ballet was an art form for the nobility. The French Revolution (1789-1799) drastically changed the political climate and power structure of France. The king, his family, and many members of the aristocracy were executed in 1793. Old ideas of aristocratic power and rule by divine right were replaced by democratic ideals such as equality and civil government. Without the support of the monarchy, ballet was in need of new patronage. While ballet could have easily disappeared in the midst of this political upheaval, it instead adapted to suit a new audience – a more democratic audience made up of members of the general public. As you might imagine, the French revolutionaries of the early 1800's were not interested in the old ballets that honored the king and reinforced political concepts such as rule by divine right. Thus a change in subject in matter is one the clear shifts that demarcates the Romantic era. Rather than kings and queens or lords and ladies, the heroes and heroines of Romantic ballet are common men and women.

Theatrically, the following changes are hallmarks of the Romantic era: the advent of the proscenium stage, the use of gas lighting, shorter and lighter costumes for female dancers, and pointe shoes that allowed female dancers to begin dancing on the tips of the toes. As we will see, the overall effect created by flickering light, ethereal costumes, and gliding dancers lent itself perfectly to the subject matter of the Romantic ballets.

While there is some debate about the first records of dancing *en pointe*, or on the tips of the toes, Marie Taglioni (1804-1884) is generally credited with being the first dancer to do so. By the 1820's, dancing en pointe was considered an important part of ballet technique. In the 1832 ballet *La Sylphide*, Taglioni appeared in a mid-calf length, bell shaped dress with a fitted and boned bodice. This style of costume became known as the Romantic tutu.

Romanticism was not just a movement in dance, but a movement in all of the arts. The Romantic Movement began in the late 1700's and reached its peak between roughly 1800 and 1840. This artistic movement was in part a reaction to the industrial revolution and involved elevating authentic, emotional experiences over practical rationalization. The Romantic artists, poets, philosophers, composers, and choreographers all explored similar subject matter. Key Romantic concepts include: interest in emotions and extreme emotional responses, a fascination with foreign cultures and exotic locales, mythical or imaginary characters, the use of natural, outdoor settings, and the concept of transcendent experience or a spiritual world.

The ballet *Giselle* is considered the archetypical Romantic ballet.

The ballet, choreographed by Jean Coralli and Jules Perrot, premiered at the Paris Opera in 1841. Consider the story of the ballet *Giselle:*

> The ballet Giselle takes place in a German village during a celebration of the grape harvest. A nobleman, Count Albrecht falls in love with a village girl, Giselle. He begins to court her, pretending to be a young peasant himself. Giselle is also courted by Hilarion, a local woodsman, who discovers that Albrecht is in fact a nobleman. A hunting party of nobles arrives midway through the first act. The party includes Albrecht's betrothed, a noblewoman named Bathilde. Bathilde, who is charmed by Giselle's beauty presents Giselle with a necklace. During the stay of the hunting party, the jealous Hilarion reveals the true identity of Albrecht. In her shock and pain over Albrecht's betrayal, the delicate Giselle goes mad and dies as the first act closes.

> Act two takes place at night in a wooded cemetery not far from the village. Hilarion comes to mourn at Giselle's grave. At midnight the spirits of the Willis, young girls who have died before their wedding days, rise up from the earth and the terrified Hilarion flees and is pursued to his death. Albrecht too comes to the fresh grave of Giselle bearing flowers, and the Willis, led by their queen, make him dance until dawn with the intension of killing him from exhaustion. The spirit of Giselle loves him still, though, and succeeds in preventing his death. Albrecht lives to see the dawn and has a last farewell to the spirit of Giselle before she returns to the grave.

How are the characteristics of Romanticism exemplified in this ballet? How are the prevailing political sentiments of nineteenth century France addressed? Now that we have discussed the general artistic concept of Romanticism, let at us look at the specific conventions associated with Romantic ballet.

At the height of the Romantic period, dancing en pointe had become an expectation for female dancers. Likewise, the Romantic tutu was the accepted and expected costume for almost all female roles. Because Romantic ballet was very literal, meaning that it was designed to tell a specific story, stage scenery was important. Also, because Romantic ballet was story-driven, pantomime and gesture were almost always used. Romantic ballets relied heavily on costume, set, and pantomime to convey the plot to the audience members. Another notable characteristic of the Romantic period is that a female star, or ballerina, became the central character in most plots. Females became the unrivaled stars of the ballet during this era, with many ballet patrons favoring specific dancers.

Two of the best known Romantic ballerinas were Marie Taglioni (1804-1884) and Fanny Elssler (1810-1884). Each of these women had a different performance style and each also had her own dedicated fan base. Taglioni was dubbed the "Christian dancer" by one journalist of the day, in contrast to Elssler, the "pagan dancer." Specifically, Taglioni was a true technician. Delicate and light on her feet, she emphasized clarity and proper execution of the ballet steps. Elssler, in contrast, had an earthy, passionate style. She was a dramatist and focused on portraying deep human emotion through her movement. Both of these dancers helped to spread the popularity of Romantic ballet beyond France. Taglioni offered more than 200 performances in Russia while Fanny Elssler spent two years touring the United States. These Romantic ballerinas reached their peak of popularity in the 1840's. Fanny Elssler's carriage was pulled by hand through the streets of New York and the United States Congress adjourned in order to attend her ballet performance.

Although France was the center of Romantic ballet, the art developed in Denmark and Russia as well. In these countries, male dancers participated equally with their female counterparts, doing more than simply providing support for the female dancers. Ballet in both Denmark and Russia was still supported by royal courts. August Bournonville (1805-1879) trained and danced with the Paris Opera and then returned to Copenhagen to serve as the director of the Royal Danish Ballet. In Russia many dancers were imported from France, but some Russian stars began to emerge during the Romantic period. Giselle was first performed in Russia one year after its Paris premiere with Elena Andreyanova, (1819-1857), as Giselle. We will see that the geographic center of ballet gradually shifted from France to Russia.

Classical Ballet (1850-1900)

As declining ticket sales and issues of patronage began to impact ballet in France in the mid 1800's, the geographic center of the art form gradually shifted from France to Russia. During this Classical Period, ballet again benefitted from royal patronage, this time from the Imperial Russian Court of the Romanovs. The Romanov tsars, in an effort to westernize their courts, invited artists from Western Europe to Russia. The most famous of these was Marius Petipa (1818-1910), a Frenchman who arrived in Russia in 1847. By 1862, Petipa had been named ballet master of the Imperial Theater in St. Petersburg. Petipa was a prolific choreographer, creating over 77 works. Petipa's name is synonymous with Classical ballet, and during this period ballet technique advanced and theatrical conventions evolved. Petipa made St. Petersburg the world center of ballet during this time period.

Petipa created spectacular choreography for women, and during the Classical period females remained the unrivaled stars of the ballet. Pointe shoes continued to be an important aspect of Classical ballet performance, and costumes for women were once again shortened. The Classical tutu is made of stiff fabric that sticks out in a circle from the dancer's hips. This tutu allows for the audience to see the dancer's legs from hip to toe. It also allows for still greater freedom of movement. Based on the patronage of the Tsar, the nobility once again was honored in the plots and staging of the Classical ballets. Most include royal characters and the convention of bowing and curtseying to these royal characters is used extensively. Just as with Romantic ballet, the plots of Classical ballets are of primary importance, and pantomime and gesture are used extensively to convey the story. Set, costume, and lighting are also used to convey and enhance the plot.

Two other dance conventions that developed during the Classical period are the Grand Pas de Deux and divertissement. The Grand Pas de Deux, or "big dance for two," was first developed during the Romantic era, but truly became a convention during the Classical ballet period. The dance between a lead male dancer and lead female dancer always follows the same format. The dance is composed of four sub-sections, which always take place in the same order: adagio, male solo, female solo, and coda. The adagio is a slower segment that sets the stage and often involves the male lifting, turning, and dipping the female. There is a lot of contact between the male and female dancers during the adagio. The male solo showcases the male dancer's athleticism, with particular emphasis placed on big leaps and turns. The female solo showcases intricate pointe work. The coda, in contrast to the adagio, is quick and lively. It often has a "call and answer" format, where the male and female dancers take turns executing difficult steps to impress the audience. The coda usually finishes with both dancers moving together in a fast, high-energy finale.

Another convention of Classical choreography is the use of a divertissement. A divertissement serves as a diversion from the primary plot, or, quite simply, extra dancing inserted into the ballet. *Sleeping Beauty*, choreographed by Petipa in 1890 to a musical score by Pyotr Ilyich Tchaikovsky, is considered one of the three most famous Russian ballets and offers perhaps the best example of a divertissement:

In the Prologue scene, the court of King Florestan is celebrating the christening of Princess Aurora. The courtiers are assembled around her cradle as the festivities begin. The king and queen enter, followed by six fairies and their cavaliers. Each fairy dances, offering her special gift to the infant princess. Suddenly, before the Lilac Fairy can present her gift, the wicked Fairy Carabosse interrupts the ceremony. Angry because she has not been invited, Carabosse delivers a curse upon the tiny princess: she will grow up to be beautiful, but one day will prick her finger and die. The Lilac Fairy intervenes, promising that the princess will but sleep until awakened by a prince's kiss.

Act I takes place during Aurora's 16th birthday party. Her father informs her that she must select one of four visiting princes as her husband. Aurora dances with the princes, each of whom offers her a rose and declares his love. As the celebration continues, the disguised Carabosse hands Aurora a bouquet in which a spindle is concealed. Aurora pricks her finger, and as she falls the Lilac Fairy appears and casts her spell, putting the entire court to sleep.

One hundred years have passed at the beginning of Act II. Prince Florimund and his hunting party stop beside a lake. As the hunt moves on the prince is left alone. To his amazement, the Lilac Fairy appears and conjures a vision of Princess Aurora. Enchanted by the vision, Prince Florimund begs the Lilac Fairy to lead him to Aurora. A boat takes them to the castle, where they are confronted by Carabosse, who turns herself into a monster. With help from the Lilac Fairy, the prince overpowers Carabosse. Once inside the castle, Prince Florimund discovers the sleeping Aurora and awakens her with a kiss.

In Act III, the divertissement, the court is celebrating the wedding of Princess Aurora and Prince Florimund. Characters from other fairy tales including Little Red Riding Hood, Puss and Boots, Little Bo Peep, and others are guests at the wedding. These characters dance to entertain the prince and princess. After Aurora and Florimund's Grand Pas De Deux, the occasion ends as the entire court joins in the finale.

As you can see, the story is basically finished at the end of Act II with the awakening kiss. Act III is a diversion, or extra dancing minimally related to the main plot. Little Red Riding Hood, for example, does nothing to further enhance the plot of *Sleeping Beauty*. Rather, these short dances are performed for the entertainment of the wedding guests (and audience). In the ballet *The Nutcracker*, the performances by the exotic holiday treats in the Land of Sweets are also examples of divertissement.

The other ballets that make up the "Big Three" include *Swan Lake* (1895) and *The Nutcracker* (1892). Like *Sleeping Beauty*, both of these ballets are performed to music by Tchaikovsky. The choreography for both is jointly attributed to Petipa and his assistant, Lev Ivanov (1834-1901). *The Nutcracker* was Petipa's conception, but was actually choreographed by Ivanov following Petipa's death. While *The Nutcracker* was not well received in Russia, it has become the most frequently staged ballet in America and a Christmas holiday tradition for many ballet companies.

As the 20th century began, people tired of Petipa's ideas and the traditions and conventions of Classical ballet. By now the Russian ballet had surpassed the French ballet and many Russian dancers had become international stars. Probably the most notable ballerina of this time was Anna Pavlova, (1881-1931). Pavlova danced at an exciting time in ballet history. She and other dancers of this period experienced the biggest changes ever to take place in ballet; they witnessed the end of the Classical period and the birth of Contemporary ballet.

Early Contemporary Ballet (1900-1950)
While the transition from the Romantic to Classical periods was precipitated largely by a shift in the geographical center of ballet, this was not the case with the transition from Classical to Contemporary ballet. During this time period, Russia remained

the world center of ballet. Rather than a change in geography, the shift to Contemporary ballet was based on changes in philosophy, or ideas and beliefs about dance as an art form. Romantic and Classical ballet look rather similar. In fact many of the specific ballets look similar to one another in terms of costuming, choreography, set, and music. This is not the case with Contemporary ballet. Contemporary ballet not only looks very different from Romantic and Classical ballet, but there is wide variation in the appearance of different pieces of Contemporary ballet choreography as well.

The early Contemporary ballet movement was largely based on questioning the conventions and traditions of Classical ballet. The Contemporary movement, in essence, was about expanding choreographic choices and allowing more options and fewer rules related to costuming, music, choreography, and set. In 1907 Mikhail Fokine (1880-1942) questioned the tradition of the Classical tutu. He felt that the look was getting stale and with his Greek-influenced ballet, *Eunice*, he costumed the dancers so that they would appear to be in bare feet. He did this by having toes painted onto the dancers' shoes; to actually dance with bare feet or legs was against the rules of the Imperial Theatre.

Like many of the Romantic artists a century before, Fokine was influenced by political unrest and disillusioned with aristocratic rule. Fokine's ideas about technique as a means to express emotion rather than to demonstrate technical proficiency, his dislike of pantomime and gesture, and his use of non-traditional costuming and musical choices laid the groundwork for the Contemporary movement, but were not well-received by the Imperial Theatre. Fokine left the Imperial Theatre in 1909 to become the first choreographer for a new ballet company, the Ballets Russes (Russian Ballet). This company was established by Sergei Diaghilev, a young member of the Russian nobility with a strong interest in the arts. Not a dancer or choreographer himself, Diaghilev served as both a patron and producer for the Ballets Russes. His goal was to share Russian art and culture with the world, and to avoid the revolutionary fervor and political unrest in Russia, he moved the company to Monte Carlo in 1911 but continued to use Russian choreographers and dancers. The Ballets Russes was primarily a touring company; they never performed in Russia.

In 1912, Diaghilev replaced Fokine as choreographer for the Ballets Russes with Vaslav Nijinsky (1889-1950). Nijinsky was a classically trained dancer who continued to question traditional ballet choreography. He used non-traditional costumes and music, parallel feet, assymetrical choreography, and eliminated pantomime and gesture. Movement, rather than plot or storyline, was now the focus of ballet. In fact, ballet during this time period looks more like modern dance than Classical ballet. What had previously been viewed as the steadfast traditions of ballet – classical music, tutus, pointe shoes, Grand Pas de Deux, storyline, realistic set - became options rather than requirements. Additionally, Contemporary choreographers began to offer shorter pieces of choreography. Often Diaghilev would present three of these one-act ballets together to create an evening length performance.

During his tenure with the Ballets Russes, Nijinsky choreographed two of the hallmark pieces of the early Contemporary ballet movement. In *Afternoon of a Faun* (1912), Nijinsky used parallel positions and realistic costumes to portray a young faun's sexually-charged fascination with a group of woodland nymphs. The sensuality of the choreography, while mild by today's standards, was shocking to the audiences of the early 20th century and a sharp contrast to the fairytale subject matter of the Classical ballets. In *Rite of Spring*, Nijinsky used a complicated and non-traditional musical score by Stravinsky to tell the story of an ancient Russian fertility ritual that involved the selection and sacrifice of a virgin who is forced to dance herself to death. While now accepted as an important piece of early Contemporary choreography, *Rite of Spring* actually created a riot among audience members at the Paris premiere. Despite being one the most influential early Contemporary choreographers, a falling out with Diaghilev and declining mental health led to Nijinsky's departure from the Ballets Russes and eventual commitment to a sanitorium.

Leonide Massine (1895 -1979) and Nijinsky's sister, Bronislava Nijinska (1891-1972), both choreographed for the Ballets Russes from 1916 until the early 1920s. In 1923 George Balanchine (1904-1983) was hired as ballet master for the Ballets Russes. Between 1923 and Diaghilev's death in 1929, Balanchine created 10 pieces for the Ballets Russes, the most famous of which are *Apollo* and *Prodigal Son*. After Diaghilev's death, Balanchine continued to work in Europe until being invited to America in 1933. There Balanchine founded the School of American Ballet in 1934 and the company that would later become the New York City Ballet in 1935. One of Balanchine's greatest contributions to dance was his concept of the plot-less ballet. Rather than convey a story, Balanchine was often interested in using dance as a visual expression of music or using choreography to study a particular style of movement. He continued the Contemporary philosophy of questioning tradition and often had dancers perform wearing simply a leotard and tights. He also eschewed the convention of the Grand Pas de Deux, preferring instead a duet that allowed both lead dancers to be on stage together in a less contrived way.

While Balanchine was instrumental in making the United States a world center for ballet, the development of American ballet was also aided by the dispersal of Diaghilev's dancers following his death. Many of these dancers put down roots throughout Europe and America, founding ballet companies and teaching

Russian ballet technique. One such dancer was Adolph Bolm (1884-1951), who settled in San Francisco in 1933 and founded the San Francisco Opera Ballet, today the San Francisco Ballet, the oldest ballet company in America.

Ballet from 1950-Present

Ballet has continued to evolve during the last half of the 20th century and into the present day. During the 1970s, some ballet companies began to perform works that blended ballet and modern dance choreography, such as Twyla Tharp's *Push Comes to Shove*. This blending of dance forms has continued in ballet and in other dance genres, and today many choreographers weave together ballet, modern dance, jazz, and world dance forms to create new and interesting dance choreography.

Sources Considered in this Chapter:

Ambrosio, Nora. *Learning About Dance.* Dubuque, IA: Kendall Hunt, 2010.

Au, Susan. *Ballet and Modern Dance.* London: Thames & Hudson, 2002.

Crisp, Clement and Edward Thorpe. *The colorful world of ballet.* London: Octopus Books, 1978.

Dodd, Craig. *Ballet.* London: Albany Books, 1979.

Homans, Jennifer. *Apollo's angels: a history of ballet.* New York: Random House, 2010.

Jonas, Gerald. *Dancing: the pleasure, power, and art of movement.* New York: Harry N. Abrams, 1992.

Kirstein, Lincoln. *Movement and metaphor: four centuries of ballet.* New York: Praeger Publishers, 1970.

Lihs, Harriet. *Appreciating Dance.* Highstown, N.J.: Princeton Book Company, 2009.

Nadel, Myron Howard and Marc Raymond Strauss. *The Dance Experience.* Highstown, N.J.: Princeton Book Company, 2003.

Chapter 6

Modern Dance

Modern dance is a twentieth century concert art form that is much less familiar than ballet to most untrained observers. The word "modern," when applied to any of the arts, often results in a controversial or unclear meaning because of its temporal association. In other words, most dance appreciation students would assume that the term modern dance refers to the popular culture dance of today. Today's popular dance forms are actually derived from the jazz dance genre, which we will discuss in Chapter 7.

Prior to the early 1900s, European and American concert dance centered on ballet. However, in the early twentieth century, new choreographers began to rebel against the rules and conventions of ballet. Although modern dance defines itself as a concert dance form, it has no direct roots in any ballet companies, schools or artists. While Loie Fuller set the stage for a new dance form with her experimental movement and lighting, the first two well-known American dancers to break away from classical ballet were Isadora Duncan and Ruth St. Denis. Although their styles differed, Duncan and St. Denis's unconventional approaches were clearly something different than ballet. In fact, early modern dance largely defines itself as a concert dance form that is not ballet. While the early pioneers of this new art form did not define themselves as modern dancers, they set the stage for a new era in dance history: the American modern dance movement of the 1920s. The pioneers Isadora Duncan, Ruth St. Denis, and Ted Shawn created works based on personal experience and used the body to express emotions such as passion, fear, joy, and grief. Rather than adhering to a set form and a limited movement vocabulary, as in ballet, these pioneers of modern dance created movements based on what they wanted to express. The movement styles of the pioneers were widely varied. The similarity between them lay in the fact that all sought to create a new concert dance form.

The Pioneers
Loie Fuller (1862-1928):
In the 1890's, Loie Fuller began experimenting with the effects of gas lighting on her loose, flowing silk costumes. Fuller was more of an inventor and theatrical staging innovator than a dancer. In fact, she had minimal dance training. She used improvisation and natural arm movements in combination with her creative lighting techniques to create staged spectacles. Her costumes included voluminous skirts that she manipulated with hidden wands for visual effect. Fuller viewed her art purely as visual entertainment. Unlike the other pioneers, she was not interested in telling stories or expressing emotions through movement.

Isadora Duncan (1877-1927):
Considered by many the founding mother of American modern dance, Isadora Duncan had studied classical ballet but found its traditions and conventions too confining. In her ideas about dance as well as in her social and political ideas, Isadora Duncan was a revolutionary. Beginning with her first performance in 1898, Duncan discarded tutus, pointe shoes, and even corsets and slippers. She danced barefoot in loose, flowing tunics. Her movements were based on the natural movements of the human body and included hopping, skipping, and swaying. Using this simple movement vocabulary, Isadora sought not to merely entertain, but to create art that expressed the human spirit and deeply felt emotions. She found the human body in motion to be an object of sublime beauty and sought to share this beauty with others. Duncan was a charismatic dancer and was

powerfully expressive in her simplistic, natural movements.

Isadora Duncan had two children with two different men, neither of whom she married. Her political leanings were considered scandalous as well, particularly after her tour of Russia resulted in pro-Bolshevik work. These scandals, in addition to her short, loose haircut, lack of corsets, and disregard for social conventions in general, helped make her famous. She used this fame and notoriety to support herself and the dance schools she established. By performing and lecturing at teas and social events of the American upper class, Duncan raised funds to support schools for Duncan-dancing in Greece, Germany, Russia, and Scandinavia. While Isadora Duncan eventually received international recognition as a concert dancer, her schools always struggled financially. After her untimely death in 1927 (her long scarf wound around the moving wheels of a convertible, breaking her neck), six of Isadora Duncan's students, the "Isadorables," continued teaching her technique and repertory.

Ruth St. Denis (1879-1968):
Ruth St. Denis was encouraged to perform from a young age. She studied ballroom and skirt dancing, or vaudeville-style dancing, and took her first job in a variety act in 1894. While Ruth St. Denis often returned to vaudeville in times of financial need, she viewed herself as a more serious artist and began to explore her interests in eastern spiritualism, ethnically-inspired dance, and musical imagery. Many of her most famous dances were inspired by Eastern cultures and mythologies, particularly those from India and Egypt. Unlike Isadora Duncan, Ruth St. Denis never developed her own movement vocabulary; rather, she borrowed movements from ballet, Duncan-dancing, and a wide variety of world dance forms including Indian, Japanese, Egyptian, and Spanish. It is important to note that her dances were not authentic representations of these world dance forms,

but rather were her impressions of the dances.

After a successful solo career, St. Denis married Ted Shawn in 1914. Together they opened the Denishawn School and Company in Los Angeles. Here St. Denis exercised her creative freedom as the driving creative force, while Ted Shawn was responsible for teaching technique and dance composition. Together they nurtured and developed the first generation of modern dancers, including such notables as Martha Graham, Doris Humphrey, and Charles Weidman. After the Denishawn marriage and partnership ended in the early 1930s, Ruth St. Denis became heavily involved in liturgical dance and choreography for movement choirs.

Ted Shawn (1891-1972):
Together with Ruth St. Denis, Ted Shawn was one of the founders of Denishawn (see above). Following their divorce, Ted Shawn taught dance at Springfield College in Massachusetts. Here he founded an all male concert dance group, Ted Shawn and His Men Dancers, in 1933. This company did much to change the view that male dancers were merely supports for their female counterparts. In addition to establishing a place for men in modern dance, Ted Shawn founded the Jacob's Pillow Dance Festival. Still held annually, it is the oldest dance festival in America.

First Generation
By the 1920s, America was ready for a new dance form. Isadora Duncan's famous Duncan-dancing and Denishawn's extensive, exotic tours had planted the seed; audiences and dancers were now open to the concept of a new, non-ballet form of serious theatrical dancing. The first generation of modern dancers began developing this art form as we know it today.

Martha Graham (1894-1991):

Martha Graham began studying at Denishawn in 1916 and, over the next seven years, had roles as a Denishawn student, teacher, and performer. She often danced as Ted Shawn's partner and was one of the best-known members of the company. Eventually frustrated by the eclectic nature and lack of specificity in Denishawn training, Graham left the company and set out on her own, giving her first independent concert in 1926.

By 1930, Martha Graham had formed her own company in New York, choreographing pieces such as *Lamentation*, which can be described as dark, heavy, and earthbound. The daughter of a psychiatrist, Graham's works often include dramatic analyses of the human psyche. Greek mythology, biblical stories, the American pioneer spirit, and psychological turmoil are themes that Graham addressed repeatedly. Graham's movement system was based on the contraction and release of the center of the body; this gave her movement a hard, angular, often abrupt look that contrasted with the smooth, graceful movements of Isadora Duncan and Ruth St. Denis. Graham created a highly specific technique to train dancers to perform her choreography. The Graham technique is now as highly codified as ballet.

A prolific and serious artist, Graham choreographed 181 dances over sixty years. She herself continued performing until the age of 76. Because the Martha Graham Company performed exclusively Graham choreography, many of her students would eventually leave to form their own companies and explore their own ideas about movement. The second generation of modern dancers includes many Graham Company alumni.

Doris Humphrey (1895-1958):

Like Martha Graham, Doris Humphrey was a student, then teacher and performer, with the Denishawn Company. Her creative abilities were quickly recognized, and she collaborated with Ruth St. Denis on music visualizations, or dances that interpreted musical structure through movement. Like Graham, Doris Humphrey was eventually disenchanted with the eclecticism of Denishawn and sought to establish a more structured modern dance technique.

After leaving Denishawn in 1828, Humphrey created a technique based on the principles of fall and recovery. This technique is interested in the play of gravity on the human body and in the ways that the body responds to gravitational pull. After giving her first independent show with Charles Weidman, the two went on to form the Humphrey-Weidman Studio and Company in New York. Her choreography often addressed human relationships, as with *Day on Earth*.

After arthritis forced an early end to Doris Humphrey's performing career, she continued to teach modern dance. She became the artistic director of her former student Jose Limon's second generation company. Her book on dance composition, *The Art of Making Dances* (1959) is still one of the premier texts on this subject.

Charles Weidman (1901-1975):
Charles Weidman was inspired to dance at the age of fifteen after seeing Ruth St. Denis on a touring performance. In 1920 he received a summer scholarship to study at Denishawn, at the end of which he was hired as a dancer for the Denishawn Company. After leaving Denishawn, he collaborated with Doris Humphrey and founded the Humphrey-Weidman Studio and Company.

Weidman was influenced by Ted Shawn, and brought a masculine approach to the new modern dance form. Wit, kinetic pantomime, and abstract movements are hallmarks of Weidman's choreography. His choreography often focused on character study or gave commentary on American life. *Lynchtown* is

Weidman's account of the lynching of an African-American man in Omaha in the 1930s. When Doris Humphrey retired from performing in 1945, the Humphrey-Weidman Company was disbanded. After struggling with severe depression for several years, Charles Weidman established the Charles Weidman Theater Dance Company and continued teaching and choreographing until his death.

Lester Horton (1906-1953):

Lester Horton received early training in both ballet and Native American dance. His Los Angeles based company, The Lester Horton Dance Group, first performed in 1932 and became known over the next two decades for its use of satire and for addressing themes of social and political protest. Horton was one of the first modern dance choreographers to cross over into choreography for commercial projects and Hollywood films. His company was also among the first to include African-American, Hispanic, and Asian dancers.

Horton's modern dance technique is based on a lengthened body line, diagonal tension, and long balances. In the Horton technique, the torso is the center of all movement. Because Horton's choreography often blended different dance forms, including ballet, modern, and world dance forms, he designed his technique to correct physical faults and to prepare dancers for any genre of dance they may wish to pursue.

Second Generation

By the 1950s the first generation modern dancers had produced a group of talented proteges who set out to develop and create their own modern dance techniques and choreography. Because modern dance was now an established art form, the second generation choreographers were not fighting to earn a place for their art. This freedom allowed them to experiment with the blending of different dance forms, humor, and personal expression through dance.

Erick Hawkins (1909-1994):
Erick Hawkins received a B.A. in classics from Harvard University before enrolling at the School of American Ballet under George Balanchine. In 1938 he joined Martha Graham's company, becoming its first male member. In addition to being the lead male dancer for the Graham Company, Hawkins was to married Martha Graham for six years. Even before they divorced, though, Hawkins began choreographing for his own company.

In establishing the Erick Hawkins Dance Company in 1951, Hawkins drew on Native American themes, celebrated natural phenomena, and made frequent use of masks. These characteristics of Hawkins choreography are clearly evident in *Plains Daybreak*. Hawkins used only original musical scores as accompaniment and strongly believed that dance accompaniment should always be performed live. His approach to movement was based on natural kinesthetic response. He developed a free-flowing technique that gave his dancing a light and fluid quality.

Paul Taylor (1930-):
Paul Taylor trained in ballet before performing in the works of Doris Humphrey, Charles Weidman, and Martha Graham. He was a soloist with Graham's company from 1955-1962, even as he choreographed and performed with his own company, which he founded in 1954. His movement style can be described as vigorous, strong, and athletic. These characteristics, along with Taylor's love of 18th century music, are evidenced in *Airs*.

Paul Taylor often uses both the grace of ballet and the power of modern dance to create engaging works. His choreography is full of juxtaposition, often contrasting light and dark, humor and tragedy, and technical virtuosity with pedestrian gestures. These contrasts lend an unpredictable quality to Taylor's choreography.

Taylor continues to choreograph today, with his 2002 *Promethean Fire* often interpreted as an artistic response to the 9/11 terror attacks.

Jose Limon (1908-1972):

Jose Limon moved to New York City in 1928; it was here that he viewed his first dance performance. Inspired by shifting perceptions of the male dancer, Limon began his study under Doris Humphrey and Charles Weidman. After 10 years of study and performance, Limon established his own dance company, the Jose Limon Dance Company, after serving in World War II.

Jose Limon's technique is closely related to the Humphrey-Weidman technique with additional emphases on balance and control. Limon further embellished the Humphrey-Weidman technique with several of his signature arm and hand gestures. Frequently exploring his Mexican-American heritage through dance, many of Limon's works are fiercely dramatic. Considered by many to be Limon's masterpiece, *The Moor's Pavane* is a dramatic portrayal of Shakespeare's *Othello*. Limon also used dance as a social and political statement in *The Traitor*, a piece of choreography that uses the Last Supper betrayal of Jesus as a metaphor for the climate of fear and mistrust created by the McCarthy Hearings in the 1950s.

Alvin Ailey (1931-1989):

Born in Texas, African-American choreographer Alvin Ailey moved to Los Angeles with his single mother when he was a teenager. He began training with Lester Horton in 1949. Ailey moved to New York in 1954 to perform in the Broadway production of *House of Flowers*. He remained in New York and studied and performed with Martha Graham, Doris Humphrey, and Charles Weidman, among others, before founding his own company in 1958.

The Alvin Ailey American Dance Theater (AAADT) began with seven dancers who performed both modern dance classics and new works created by Ailey and other young artists. Many of Ailey's choreographic works are devoted to African-American themes. Ailey frequently used what he called his "blood memories" of Texas, the blues, spirituals and gospel as inspiration. These elements are all evident in *Revelations*, the 1960 work that has become the signature piece of the AAADT. Alvin Ailey's use of personal experiences makes his choreography extremely accessible to audiences. Ailey was also one of the first modern dance choreographers to begin blending modern dance with ballet and other world dance forms. Although Alvin Ailey created 79 works over his lifetime, he maintained that his company was not exclusively a repository for his own work. AAADT performs work by a variety of other choreographers and has provided opportunities for many other African-American choreographers.

Post-Modernism

By the 1960s modern dance was well-established as a concert art form and the dance world was ready for the next revolution. Just as the pioneers of modern dance revolted against the perceived restrictions of ballet, the post-modern choreographers of the 1960s and 70s revolted against the perceived restrictions of modern dance. Like art, music, and other cultural phenomenon of the time, postmodern dance was a rebellion against traditional ideas and assumptions. Postmodernists questioned the established parameters of dance and pushed dance and art to new levels. They questioned not only the need for meaning in dance, but went so far as to question the need for dance technique. The postmodern movement was short-lived, but by breaking all of the rules it opened the door for the blended, collaborative, innovative dance and performance art of the 21st century.

Merce Cunningham (1919-2009):

Chronologically, Cunningham would be considered a second generation modern dance choreographer. Because his ideas about dance were so radically different, though, he is included here. Considered by many the father of post-modernism, Cunningham questioned the modern dance idea that dance should have meaning. He was fascinated by watching the human body in motion. Like many of the post-modern choreographers, Cunningham did not believe that only trained dancers were interesting to watch; he was fascinated even by pedestrian movement. He did use trained dancers in his choreography, though, and believed that dance performers required a solid technical base in order to be clear in their movements. He believed that all the body's movements could constitute dance if placed in the appropriate context.

From 1939 to 1945, Cunnigham was a soloist with the Martha Graham Dance Company. During that time, he began to choreograph independently, presenting his first New York solo concert in 1944. After establishing the Merce Cunningham Dance Company in 1953, he choreographed over one hundred and fifty works. Frequently collaborating with the avant garde composer John Cage, Merce Cunningham experimented with the relationship between dance and music and created choreography that was unrelated to the music that accompanied it. The music and dance were created independently and only brought together for performance, with dancers often rehearsing with stop watches instead of music prior to the actual performance. In order to ensure that his choreography did not impose a set meaning on the audience members and was not subconsciously or emotionally influenced, Cunningham used two methods: chance and indeterminacy. Chance involved actions such as flipping a coin to determine which of two possible movement phrases would be used in a dance. Indeterminacy was a sort of structured improvisation that allowed the dancers to make unique choices about speed, direction, and other aspects of the dance during each specific performance. Cunningham used a Zen-like approach to dance interpretation, believing that the universe (through chance) and the audience members would make their own meaning; he did not want to impose any meaning on his work or on audiences.

Yvonne Rainer (1934 -):
Born and raised in San Francisco, Yvonne Rainer moved to New York in 1956. Between 1959 and 1960, she studied modern dance at the Martha Graham School and ballet at Ballet Arts. In the early 1960s, she attended classes taught by Merce Cunningham, where she met a number of her future collaborators. In 1962, she became a founding member of the Judson Dance Theatre. This collective of postmodern choreographers favored alternative performance spaces, music, costuming, and generally questioned all of the previously accepted norms of concert dance.

Much like other choreographers of her era, Rainer sought to blur the line separating dance movement from non-dance movement. She favored including artists of other disciplines in her choreography, and favored using the "everyday body" as opposed to the performing body. This meant that her dancers performed choreographed movements with a mundane attitude, minimizing the dramatic aspects of dance.Ranier often choreographed based on a series of generic tasks that integrated everyday gestures into a dance vocabulary (walking, running, lifting, etc.). In *Trio A*, Ranier questions yet another dance convention - the use of music.

Twyla Tharp (1941-):
Twyla Tharp was born in 1941 in Portland, Indiana, and in 1951 she moved with her family to Rialto, California, where her

parents opened a drive-in movie theater. Tharp's mother was a piano teacher and began teaching Twyla as a toddler. As a child, she also studied ballet, tap, jazz, acting, and the violin. Transferring to Barnard College in New York as a college sophomore, Tharp studied with Martha Graham and Merce Cunningham. After graduating with a degree in art history in 1963, Tharp joined the Paul Taylor Dance Company. Only two years later, in 1965, she founded Twyla Tharp Dance. Twyla came of age as a dancer during the postmodern period, and her early work is decidedly abstract and pedestrian.

Unlike many of the postmodern choreographers who continued in film, performance art, or in other avant-garde outlets after the end of the postmodern era, Twyla transitioned to a more mainstream style of choreography. Twyla began blending the pedestrian, gestural style of postmodernism with ballet, jazz, and even tap dance. In *Sinatra Suite*, Tharp blends ballet, ballroom dance, and gesture to tell the story of the phases of a couple's relationship. Twyla Tharp's transition from postmodern rebel to one of the most accessible choreographers of the late 20th-early 21st century makes her, in many ways, a metaphor for the entire modern dance movement. By throwing out all of the rules associated with dance choreography, the postmoderners allowed future choreographers to decide for themselves which rules and conventions to apply. On a personal level, this same transition from no rules to selective application of the rules happened very clearly in the choreography of Twyla Tharp. An extremely versatile choreographer, Tharp has created works for ballet companies, modern dance companies, Broadway, and film.

Modern Dance into the 21st Century
Over time, modern dance has reconciled itself to other more traditional dance forms. Today's choreographers use a broader range of techniques, styles, and source materials than ever before. The lines separating modern dance from ballet, jazz, and world

dance forms are becoming increasingly blurred. Technological innovations including lighting, set and costume design, and innovative computer-enhanced effects are also important influences on the modern dance of today.

Mark Morris (1956-):

Born in Seattle, Mark Morris was inspired to dance after attending a performance of the Spanish flamenco at the age of eight. By age 11, Morris was performing professionally. After performing, choreographing, and studying in Spain as a teenager, Morris moved to New York City in 1976. There he studied and performed both ballet and modern dance, and in 1980 he established his own company.

In the late 1980s, Morris and his company spent three years in Belgium. It was here that he choreographed *The Hard Nut*, a non-traditional, humorous version of *The Nutcracker*. Like many of his pieces, *The Hard Nut* was both innovative and, to some, controversial. In 1990, Morris and famed ballet dancer Mikhail Baryshnikov established the White Oak Dance Project. Morris continued to create works for the White Oak Dance Project until 1995. Since 2001 the Mark Morris Dance Group has been permanently located in Brooklyn, New York. Noted for his musicality, wit, and humor, Mark Morris has also choreographed for numerous ballet companies, including the American Ballet Theatre, the San Francisco Ballet, and Les Grands Ballets Canadiens.

Pilobolus (est. 1971):

The modern dance company Pilobolus was founded by a group of Dartmouth College students in 1971. The original Pilobolus artists were Alison Chase, the instructor of the class, Robby Barnett, Martha Clarke, Lee Harris, Moses Pendleton, and Jonathan Wolken. None of the original student members had any dance training before they began to choreograph. While dancers have come and gone over the years, the company is generally comprised of about six dancers. The founding members choreographed collectively and also collaborated with the new dancers brought into the company in subsequent years. Much of the Pilobolus choreography is rooted in improvisation, weight-sharing, and in the use of novel and sometimes humorous props.

Pilobolus performances are usually technically and athletically astounding. There is extensive physical interaction and weight-sharing between the performers and exaggerations or contortions of the human form. Pilobolus Dance Theatre, based in Connecticut, has a repertory of over 100 works and is on the cutting edge in the use of lighting and computer-enhanced stage effects and graphics.

As you can see from the choreography discussed above, modern dance today mirrors our changing society in many ways. Mark Morris's *The Hard Nut* clearly questions gender roles/identities, a topic that remains timely in the 21st century. Just as technology has impacted almost all facets of our daily life, we can see the impact of technology on dance and performance art with the choreography of Pilobolus. As rules, traditions, and conventions have been questioned in society at large, they have been questioned in dance choreography as well. The lines that separate one dance genre from another have become increasingly blurred. Much of our concert dance in the 21st century is simply that – dance.

Sources Considered in this Chapter:

Ambrosio, Nora. *Learning About Dance.* Dubuque, IA: Kendall Hunt, 2010.

Anderson, Jack. *Art Without Boundaries.* Iowa City: University of Iowa Press, 1997.

Au, Susan. *Ballet and modern dance.*London: Thames & Hudson, 2002.

Jonas, Gerald. *Dancing: the pleasure, power, and art of movement.* New York: Harry N. Abrams, 1992.

Lihs, Harriet. *Appreciating Dance.* Highstown, N.J.: Princeton Book Company, 2009.

Martin, John. *The modern dance.*New York: Dance Horizons, 1933.

Mazo, Joseph. *Prime Movers.* Highstown, N.J.: Princeton Book Company, 2000.

McDonagh, Don. *The complete guide to modern dance.*Garden City, N.Y.: Doubleday, 1976.

McDonagh, Don. *The rise and fall of modern dance.*New York: Outerbridge&Dienstfrey, 1970.

Nadel, Myron Howard and Marc Raymond Strauss.*The dance experience.*Highstown, N.J.:Princeton Book Company, 2003.

Pease, Esther. *Modern Dance.* Dubuque, IA: Wm. C. Brown Company, 1966.

Chapter 7

African-Based Dance Forms (Jazz and Tap)

Just as the roots of ballet are in the court dance of seventeenth century France, the roots of jazz and tap dance are in African dance. In 1619, the first Africans were brought to America, and over the next two and a half centuries over 20 million enslaved Africans arrived in the Americas. While these captives brought with them little material evidence of their cultural identities and traditions, their music and dance have had a lasting impact on these art forms in America.

When slaves first arrived in America, Caucasian plantation owners were immediately fascinated by the wild and expressive dances of the African slaves. While the ritual functions of African dance were quickly banned by the plantation owners, the dances evolved to serve a more social function. Slaves danced to entertain each other, to compete with one another, and for personal enjoyment and expression. Social dancing in Europe, and then America, was performed with a stiff upright posture, and couples danced arm-in-arm or in a face to face embrace. Movement was limited to the legs and feet and was often stilted and contrived. This stood in stark contrast to the movements of African tribal dancing, which involved crouched, bent-knee positions and extensive use of the pelvis and torso. The following defining characteristics of African dance evident in both jazz dance and tap dance:

- Movement of the entire body, including the shoulders and hips.
- Angular bending of the arms, legs, and torso.
- Shuffling, stamping, and hopping.
- Asymmetrical fluid movement.
- An orientation into the earth [giving into gravity versus fighting against it].
- An element of competition.
- Improvisation.
- Pantomime.

History of Jazz Dance

As African culture evolved into African American culture, the characteristics of African dance evolved into African American dance styles. One of the earliest examples of this evolution, the Cakewalk, incorporated the art of pantomime. Originating in Florida, the Cakewalk was a pantomimed parody of the Caucasian upper class plantation owners going about their daily business. Much bowing and bending were characteristic of the dance, which involved couples lining up to form an aisle, then taking turns high-stepping down the line. In many instances the Cakewalk was a competition. The dance would be held at the master's house on the plantation and he would serve as judge. The Cakewalk was the sole organized and allowable forum for servants to mock their masters. The dance's name comes from the cake that would be awarded to the winning couple.

The Cakewalk may have been the first American dance to cross over from African American society to mainstream white society. By the 1890s, the Cakewalk was one of America's most popular dance styles with competitions, shows, and sheet music written specifically for its performance. While its popularity died out between 1915 and the early 1920s, it was soon replaced by other African American dance styles that included the Charleston and Black Bottom.

The Charleston originated with African Americans living on a small island near Charleston, South Carolina, though its origins can be traced back to West Africa. The Charleston as it is known today was performed as early as 1903, and by 1913 it was performed on the stages of supper clubs in Harlem. Just like the Cakewalk, the Charleston crossed over into White society and became the defining dance of the Roaring Twenties. The Charleston is also an important component in the early evolution of swing dance.

The Black Bottom originated in New Orleans in the early 1900s. It was unique in that it could be performed as a solo or by a couple. The Black Bottom, which includes African dance characteristics such as hopping, stamping, slapping the body, and moving the torso and pelvis, is considered one of the clearest links between African dance and today's tap and jazz dancing. The Black Bottom was introduced to mainstream America in 1919 through sheet music that included instructions on how to perform the dance, and by 1926 the Black Bottom had replaced the Charleston as the popular social dance of the day. Like the Charleston, the Black Bottom was a major influence on the Lindy Hop and swing dance.

By the mid-1920s, Ragtime Jazz and other popular jazz music provided rhythms and tempos that perfectly accompanied the fast footwork and kicks of the Charleston and the Black Bottom. In these early days of the Harlem Renaissance, dancers' efforts to out shine one another on the dance floor led couples to "break-away" from each other in what would become the jazz/tap tradition. This individualized break-away is at the heart of modern swing dancing.

The Savoy Ballroom, in many ways the center of jazz dance during the Harlem Renaissance, opened its doors in 1926. The Savoy featured two bandstands and a retractable stage. As the most popular dance venue in Harlem, the Savoy showcased all of the greatest artists of early jazz and swing. Famous musicians such as Cab Calloway, Count Basie and Duke Ellington would trade sets from opposite bandstands in a battle of the bands while dancers competed against one another with the newly developed break-away steps of swing dance. By 1927, following Charles Lindbergh's famous non-stop flight from the United States to Paris, this new dance style was dubbed the Lindy Hop.

The fact that the Savoy was one of the first integrated dance venues undoubtedly helped the Lindy Hop cross over to mainstream America very quickly. At a time when other ballrooms and dance halls were racially segregated, as many as 15% of the dancers at the Savoy were generally Caucasian. Soon downtown socialites and powerful New Yorkers were requesting Lindy Hoppers as performers at parties and balls. Herbert "Whitey" White, an African American former boxer and bouncer at the Savoy quickly recognized a business opportunity. Aside from being a capable businessman, Whitey also had an eye for talent and a knack for mentoring young dancers. Throughout 1930s he employed the top dancers from the Savoy, who were known as Whitey's Lindy Hoppers.

Lindy Hop swing dancing began to lose its popularity toward the end of World War II. It was replaced by new popular social dance forms such as East Coast Swing, the Jitterbug, the Jive, and Shag. This evolution in jazz dance was due, in large part, to the evolution of popular music. With the decline of the Lindy Hop, the growth of jazz dance as a professional dance form began. During the 1940s, jazz dance was influenced by both ballet and modern dance. By blending the original African-derived elements discussed earlier in this chapter with the classical technique of ballet and the natural, free expression of modern dance, jazz dance developed its own artistic quality. Unlike early jazz dance, which was performed by talented entertainers without formal training, modern jazz dance was performed by professionals trained in ballet and modern dance.

During the 1960's, two names emerged among the ranks of professional jazz dance greats: Luigi (Eugene Louis Facciuto) and Gus Giordano. Luigi developed his technique as a result of an auto accident that left him paralyzed on the right side. Doctors claimed he would never walk, much less dance, again. After operations and physical therapy, Luigi's study of the human body based on dance movement led to him not only walking again, but dancing and teaching as well. The Luigi technique is influenced by ballet and, while graceful, requires that the body be exercised and conditioned to develop strength and muscle control. Gus Giordano's jazz dance style is classical but also influenced by the natural and free body movements of modern dance. His technique uses isolations, and emphasizes movements of the head and torso.

In the 1970s, Bob Fosse became one of the most famous names in jazz dance. Fosse performed on Broadway and in films but, lacking formal dance training, his technical skill was limited. Fosse's true success was as a jazz dance choreographer. Fosse's choreographic style was distinct, highly creative and often included very sensual movements. His costume choices were often erotic, too. His choreography includes the films *All That Jazz* and *Sweet Charity*, and the Broadway hit *Dancin'*, among many other famous works. He choreographed a reproduction of *Chicago* in 1975. Fosse's style continued to influence both Broadway and Hollywood throughout the 1980s.

Jazz Dance Today

Today jazz dance encompasses many popular sub-genres of dance including breakdancing and hip-hop. Jazz dance forms continue to blur the lines between social and concert dance and between popular art and fine art. The African dance roots of jazz, though, are still evident in jazz dance today.

Beginning in the 1960s in tough neighborhoods of New York City, breakdancing emerged not as an entertainment form, but as a form of competition. As West African immigrants settled in the South Bronx, breakdancing served as a means of attaining street superiority; it was an alternative to gang warfare and physical fights. Sub-categories of breakdancing include breaking (specific moves done on or close to the floor); freestyle (gymnastic moves and partner lifts); electric boogie (flowing movements that enter one part of the body and exit another); popping (any staccato movement); and floating (steps such as the moonwalk, in which the feet seem to float across the floor). All of these dance styles can be traced to the West African cultures of Mali, Gambia, and Senegal. In the 1980s, breakdancing became part of mainstream American dance culture.

The 1980s also saw the introduction of MTV, a new medium for professional dance. When MTV began broadcasting in 1981, music videos combined high-energy jazz, street dance and social dance in visually interesting ways. Some major choreographers of the period include Michael Peters, Paula Abdul, Madonna, and Janet Jackson. The best-known music video star of the 1980s was Michael Jackson, who had a major impact on the direction of jazz dance into the new millennium. It is important to note, though, that much of Jackson's video choreography, including *Thriller*, was done by Michael Peters.

In the 1990s, popular jazz dance forms included street dancing, street funk, and hip hop. Street dance is inner city dance taken directly from the street corners with performers using boom boxes as their accompaniment. The *Fly Girls* dancers featured on the early 1990s hit show *In Living Color*, gave many primetime viewers their first look at street dance, a style of jazz which mixed street moves with technical ballet and jazz. Hip hop dance, which is performed to hip hop music, includes complex footwork, body isolations, breakdancing and gymnastic moves. Hip hop is a style of clothing, attitude, dance and music.

Jazz dance in the new century continues to look both back to the classics and forward to creative new dance styles. The current jazz dance performance world has sought a wider variety of performance platforms, including cabaret and lounge shows, cruise ship entertainment, and touring dance companies. Music videos, major television productions, and popular movies still primarily use jazz dance. The history of jazz dance has evolved along with the music and moods of each decade. Today jazz dance continues to blend the technical requirements of dance as a fine art with the social elements of popular art, making it a dance form with a wide appeal to American audiences.

History of Tap Dance
Tap dance shares many of the same African roots as jazz dance and, like jazz dance, frequently includes elements of both improvisation and competition. The other roots of tap dance, though, are in Irish dance.

During the mid-1800's, just as many newly freed slaves were heading to the industrial centers of the Northern United States, many Irish immigrants came to America to escape the Irish Potato Famine. They arrived in America through the same large port cities that provided industrial and manufacturing job opportunities to the newly relocated former slaves. Both groups were poor and struggling and found housing in the slums of New York, Philadelphia, and Boston.

Just like the African slaves before them, the Irish immigrants brought with them their own dance rhythms and steps. Irish dance is very percussive and strong; it involves the feet striking the floor forcefully enough to produce a sound. The other key characteristic of Irish dance is a very erect spine. This blending of strong, very erect Irish dancing with the looser rhythmic patterns of African dance was the beginning of tap dance. The next 60 years or so would see a fusion of cultures; the development of blues and jazz music alongside percussive dance. By the 1920s tap was well-established as its own dance genre, just in time for the Harlem Renaissance.

Tap dance reached its peak of popularity from 1920 to 1935, at the peak of the Harlem Renaissance. By the 1920s tap had become established as a distinct dance form and drew large audiences to venues such as Harlem's Cotton Club, where African American dancers and musicians performed for exclusively Caucasian audiences. During this time period, tap was performed on Broadway, in nightclubs, and in vaudeville productions. The best known tap dancer of the era was Bill ("Bojangles") Robinson, who performed on stage as well as on film. Known for his clean footwork and for dancing up on his toes with minimal heel taps, his dances were graceful and light. His rhythmic patterns also set new standards, and his phrasing is still considered the classical structure of tap. As seen in the 1935 movie *The Little Colonel* with Shirley Temple, Bojangles brought the stair dance to such a level of excellence that, to this day, it remains linked to his name. Another famous performer, John W. Bubbles (John "Bubber" Sublett) is known as the father of rhythm tap. Bubbles brought tap down from the toes and slapped his heels against the floor. He added a new range of syncopated accents to the rhythmical structure of tap. This rhythm tap style continues to be widely used in tap performances today.

By the 1940s, tap performance was transitioning from live performance to Hollywood films. Classic movies of the 1930s and 1940s showcased the great tap dancers of the day. The film industry at this time was heavily segregated, resulting in different tap dance styles being marketed to different demographics. For example, Robinson, Bubbles and the Nicholas Brothers, all African-American performers, performed an improvisational and percussive jazz style, whereas the Caucasian musical theater stars Gene Kelly and Fred Astaire utilized more ballroom and ballet-based techniques typical of Broadway.

Tap Dance Today

By the 1950s and 1960s, tap dance was in decline, but the 1970s and 80s brought a revival of this dance form. During the 1980s, tap dancing was featured in films such as *White Nights*, *The Cotton Club*, and *Tap*. Additionally, the 1980s saw the emergence of young tap dance prodigy Savion Glover, who first performed on Broadway as a 9-year-old in *The Tap Dance Kid*. Glover introduced hip hop rhythms to tap in the 1990s with his award-winning Broadway production *Bring in Da Noise, Bring in Da Funk*. Since then he has choreographed for film, commercial television, and for the 2002 Winter Olympics.

Tap dance continues to be a popular form of dance and is still frequently used in Broadway choreography. Like other dance forms, tap continues to evolve and to blur the lines between different dance genres. In addition to picking up technical influences from ballet and jazz dance, tap dance choreographers have continued the exploration of hip-hop culture that Savion Glover began in the 1990s. Tap dance continues the tradition of African-based percussive dance in the modern era.

Sources Considered in this Chapter:

Ambrosio, Nora. *Learning About Dance*. Dubuque, IA: Kendall Hunt, 2010.

"American Studies at the University of Virginia."
Web.3Apr.2013
http://xroads.virginia.edu/~ug03/lucas/cake.html

Driver, Ian. *A Century of Dance*. Great Britain: Octopus Publishing Group Ltd, 2000.

Frank, Rusty. *Tap*. New York: William Morrow & Company, 1990.

Glass, Barbara. *African American dance*.Jefferson, NC: McFarland & Company, 2007.

Haskins, James. *Black dance in America: a history through its people*. New York: Harper Collins, 1990.

Jonas, Gerald. *Dancing: the pleasure, power, and art of movement*. New York: Harry N. Abrams, 1992.

Lihs, Harriet. *Appreciating Dance*. Highstown, N.J.: Princeton Book Company, 2009.

Malone, Jacqui. *Steppin' on the Blues: the visible rhythms of African American dance*. Chicago: Uiniversity of Illinois Press, 1996.

Stearns, Marshall and Jean. *Jazz dance: the story of American vernacular dance*. New York: Macmillan Company, 1968.